PHENO

MW00586368

The MIT Press Essential Knowledge Series

A complete list of the titles in this series appears at the back of this book.

PHENOMENOLOGY

CHAD ENGELLAND

The MIT Press | Cambridge, Massachusetts | London, England

© 2020 Massachusetts Institute of Technology

All rights reserved. No part of this book may be reproduced in any form
by any electronic or mechanical means (including photocopying, recording,
or information storage and retrieval) without permission in writing from
the publisher.

This book was set in Chaparral Pro by New Best-set Typesetters Ltd. Printed
and bound in the United States of America.

Library of Congress Cataloging-in-Publication Data

Names: Engelland, Chad, author.
Title: Phenomenology / Chad Engelland.
Description: Cambridge, Massachusetts : The MIT Press, 2020. | Series:
   The MIT press essential knowledge series | Includes bibliographical
   references and index.
Identifiers: LCCN 2019055200 | ISBN 9780262539319 (paperback)
Subjects: LCSH: Phenomenology.
Classification: LCC B829.5 .E54 2020 | DDC 142/.7—dc23
LC record available at https://lccn.loc.gov/2019055200

10 9 8 7 6 5 4 3 2

The greatest step that our time has to take is to realize that with the correct sense of philosophical intuition, the phenomenological grasp of essences, a boundless field of work becomes visible.

—Edmund Husserl

CONTENTS

SERIES FOREWORD

The MIT Press Essential Knowledge series offers accessible, concise, beautifully produced pocket-size books on topics of current interest. Written by leading thinkers, the books in this series deliver expert overviews of subjects that range from the cultural and the historical to the scientific and the technical.

In today's era of instant information gratification, we have ready access to opinions, rationalizations, and superficial descriptions. Much harder to come by is the foundational knowledge that informs a principled understanding of the world. Essential Knowledge books fill that need. Synthesizing specialized subject matter for nonspecialists and engaging critical topics through fundamentals, each of these compact volumes offers readers a point of access to complex ideas.

PREFACE

When I was sixteen I got glasses for the first time. Stunning it was to experience the world in high definition again—I distinctly recall the shock of being able to see the *individual blades* of grass. With the vividness of things crying out for recognition, I was pulled into perception with a renewed intensity.

Sherlock Holmes was on one occasion accused of possessing an almost magical insight. "You appeared to read a good deal upon her which was quite invisible to me," says Watson. Holmes corrects him: "*Not invisible but unnoticed,* Watson. You did not know where to look, and so you missed all that was important. I can never bring you to realize the importance of sleeves, the suggestiveness of thumb-nails, or the great issues that may hang from a boot-lace."[1] Like good detective work, phenomenology enhances perception so that we notice all that is important in what seems to be small.

Martin Heidegger recalls how phenomenology drew him in: "I remained so fascinated by Husserl's work that I read in it again and again in the years to follow without gaining sufficient insight into what *fascinated* me. The spell emanating from the work extended to the outer appearance of the sentence structure and the title page."[2] The word *fascinate* comes from the Latin word that means "to be under a spell." Even Pope John Paul II, who as a university professor published a work of phenomenology, says, "I thank God for having allowed me also to participate in this *fascinating* enterprise."[3] Phenomenology exercises a strange and powerful hold on its participants. They are bedazzled, beguiled, bewitched.

Often things fascinate us by snatching us away from our surroundings. An addictive video game, for example, makes us insensitive to the ordinary things and people about us. In this way, what fascinates makes our world smaller; it confines us to what enthralls or enslaves. By contrast, phenomenology rekindles the magic of the ordinary by putting us back in touch with experience. Instead of making the world smaller, it opens us up to everything and everyone. It is a spell that undoes the deadening spell of the mundane allowing us to see things again as if for the first time. Maurice Merleau-Ponty puts it this way: "True philosophy entails learning to see the world anew."[4] Phenomenology fascinates by restoring charm to the things of this world. It captures our hearts by setting us free, free to experience deeply the truth of things together with others.

ACKNOWLEDGMENTS

Philosophy is there for the taking only because others have given their lives to the task of keeping it a live possibility for us, and we owe them a world of thanks. Among my many teachers, I would mention in particular Robert Sokolowski, whose courses and writings on phenomenology are rightly legendary.

I am fortunate to be at a place rich in phenomenological thinking, and my colleagues and institution deserve special mention. I was able to complete this book in a timely fashion due to support provided by Jonathan J. Sanford, Joshua Parens, and Matthew Walz. Three colleagues—Chris Mirus, Bill Frank, and Hannah Venable—were generous and insightful with their criticisms of the text. An alumnus, Jason Baxter, provided invaluable suggestions. Phenomenology has a long history at the University of Dallas, and I am glad to be able to make my own contribution to it.

I am thankful to friends, family members, students, and colleagues, who have showed me the need for this book, and who, on many occasions, have served as the first audience for my thoughts—thoughts which, often enough, are responses to the experiences I have been fortunate enough to share with them.

My wife Isela and four kids ever challenge me to see the world anew, and they are the original catalysts for filling in the theses of phenomenology with living, quivering experience.

TO THE THINGS THEMSELVES

What is it about the beach that draws us so powerfully? Here in the great expanse where the land meets the water and the water converges on the sky, there is much to take in. Taste the salt on your tongue. Smell the heavy scent of the sea breeze. Feel the radiating sun above and the gritty sand below. See the froth of the rhythmic waves. Hear their noisy crash and whispering retreat. Unlike the neutral space of the modern office, this is a total body experience, which propels us into an array of playful activities—sunbathing, beachcombing, sandcastle building, surfing, and so on.

Amid such activity, there is much to think about. If you want to learn about the tides and the forces of the ocean, turn to oceanography and physics. If you find curious the creatures that waddle about at water's edge, turn to naturalists and field biologists. If you marvel at the beauty of the spectacular colors dancing on the waves as the sun slides toward the horizon, turn to the poet or painter. If you find your heart soar beyond all expectations, look to the mystic or theologian for direction. But if you want to know how truth is at play in the ocean-side experience, turn to phenomenology.

Phenomenology is the experience *of experience*. It names both a contemporary philosophical method and a contemporary philosophical movement that follows this method. Founded by Edmund Husserl, expounded by Max Scheler, Martin Heidegger, Maurice Merleau-Ponty, and others, phenomenology is now an international movement of researchers devoted to exhibiting the truth of experience. Rather than resting content with prior conceptions, it ventures forth into the field of experience so that truth might be met in the flesh.

Beware: the book in your hands has a peculiar subject matter. It is not about this topic or that one but about *everything at all*, and that might seem to be too ambitious, especially for such a small book. But it is not about everything full stop but about everything *as experienced*. If biology is the study of life (*bios*), phenomenology would seem to be the study of appearance (*phenomenon*). What's misleading about this analogy is that the study of appearance suggests that we are dealing with *mere* appearance as opposed to reality, with a mental image instead of the existent thing. But it is just this misunderstanding of appearance that makes phenomenology so urgently necessary. Phenomenology is the study of experience, of the way things appear to us together in their truth. Sometimes there can be mere appearance; it looks like the turtle is dead but it turns out it was just playing dead, or it looks like a turtle but really it's just a curiously shaped stone. But we are able to have mere appearance because experience is fundamentally reliable; we know the turtle is in fact alive, because we now see it swimming away, or we pick up what we think is a turtle only to discover the lifeless solidity of rock. The unfolding of experience allows us to sort true appearances from mere appearances. Phenomenology does not study mere appearance; it studies the true appearance of things.

What's Absent from the Scientific Picture?

Now it might seem that phenomenology has no place in what physicists Stephen Hawking and Leonard Mlodinow refer to as the "grand design," that is, a comprehensive account of the cosmos and everything in it. Indeed, they boldly proclaim that "philosophy is dead."[1] They think it falls to science to answer the traditional big questions, and they endeavor to provide "a new picture of the universe and our place in it."[2]

The cosmos generates a bewildering variety of possible universes, but we find ourselves in the one we do because most of the other scenarios would make it impossible for us to exist. Hawking and Mlodinow comment, "Thus *our presence* selects out from this vast array only those universes that are compatible with our existence."[3] What account can they give of this presence? Owing to the inviolability of physical law, they conclude that "we are no more than biological machines."[4] Our perception and understanding take place in our brains, which work up a model of the external world. As a result, we are never really present to anything: "what one means when one says 'I see a chair' is merely that one has used the light scattered by the chair to build a mental image or model of the chair."[5] Hawking and Mlodinow give us a picture of ourselves in which we are confined to our brains.

The problem with such a picture is that it cannot accommodate the very thing we want to have pictured, namely, our place in the whole.[6] Why not? A picture looks from the outside at what it depicts, but there can be no picture of the act of looking itself, for to look inextricably involves an inside. As chapter 2 will show, there is no way to picture the presence one presently enjoys; instead, one must live one's point of view from within and come back to it through a new modality of experience. This book will unfold from this new modality, and chapter 9 will explain the method in some detail.

Our natural curiosity allows us to transcend the tiny slice of cosmic space and time that we occupy. Hawking and Mlodinow write, "We wonder, we seek answers."[7] They point out that we ask questions about the essences of things, about their existence, and about the divine, and this wonderment gives rise to science. It is just this wonderment, however, that gets left out of the picture that they sketch. As chapter 8 will show, when we wonder about something we do so by profiling that thing's presence against the absence of other possibilities. We wonder why the cosmos began with a bang because we realize it might have begun with a whimper. To make sense of wonder, then, we have to think seriously about the interplay of presence and absence. what's there & what isn't

In giving an account of the whole and our place in it, Hawking and Mlodinow must make use of concepts they cannot explain—presence and wonder—but also related terms such as speech and truth. We might say, "Ah, but these human concepts are of only subjective importance, unlike the objective, mathematical reasoning of science." But as obvious a point as it is, it must nonetheless be made: there would be no science if there were no scientists. And there would be no scientists without the peculiarly human way of wondering why something is the way it is rather than another, and this very act of wondering, which gives rise to science, is unthinkable apart from a general account of presence and the way we are able to experience and express the truth of things. The blind spot of contemporary science, an inability to locate itself in the picture it generates, serves as a primary focus for the field of philosophy called phenomenology. No account of the whole can be complete if it doesn't account for the accounting of the whole, that is, if it doesn't make sense of our curious wonder about the whole. And no account of wonder can be complete if it doesn't explain the presence of perception, not as the juxtaposition of two things, but instead as our openness to a field of experience.

Becoming a Thoughtful Spectator

How can we wonder about presence as such? The answer is phenomenology's *transcendental reduction*. It is called "transcendental," because it focuses on the *relational structure* of experience rather than any of experience's content. "Transcendence" means to "step beyond," and our experience steps beyond ourselves and runs up against things. It is called a "reduction," because it *traces back* something we experience to the experience that makes it present. The point of the transcendental reduction is to step back, to retrace the steps that make experience happen. The shift from experiencing things to *experiencing how* we experience things is very strange, but it is anticipated by some ordinary life experiences.

Introducing baseball to a child for the first time is difficult, because the novice sees without understanding and does not know how to make sense of the game. Why is the person running? Why are people cheering? What's going on? One and the same event happens in front of us, but the child cannot experience what we experience. The producer of a televised game performs much of the understanding for the viewer; the camera doesn't duplicate the experience of being in the stands; instead, it zeroes in, from the most appropriate angle, and shows the viewer the tiny corner of the field where the action is. And unlike the global view of the fan in the stadium, the shift from camera to camera helps the television viewer stay with the action.[8] The radio broadcast must be even more explicit about understanding for the viewer. What the announcer relays is not simply how things look (what even the untutored child can see); the play by play involves relating the *understanding* of what is seen. "The runner is leading off the base. The pitcher is winding up, the runner is going, the catcher is making the throw, the second baseman's got the ball, and the runner is . . ." To try to explain baseball to neophytes, to produce the experience for a televised audience, or to narrate the experience for an absent audience involves a shift into being a spectator who focuses not only on the game but also on how the game is experienced.

To enter into phenomenology is analogous to becoming a spectator in baseball. In phenomenology, one thoughtfully experiences experience in general. One can thereby analyze the fundamental structures of experience that hold for watching not only a ballgame but also a performance, a movie, or two spider monkeys swinging from branch to branch at the zoo. One can articulate the difference between seeing something and understanding what is seen. One can identify the difference between seeing with understanding and understanding without seeing (as when I simply tell you about what I saw on my trip to the zoo). To make the transcendental turn is to become a spectator to experience, who takes in the game of experience with understanding and can thereby articulate it for others. We become what Husserl calls "a nonparticipating spectator, surveyor of the world."[9] Like the spectator to baseball, the spectator to experience remains deeply engaged; the difference is that the spectator pays attention to points of view and the new dimension of understanding or intending what is seen as what it is.

A closer natural analogue to phenomenology might be sitting on a jury. During the selection process, the attorneys and the judge instruct the jurors to set aside their prejudices or pre-judgments. Their job is to take in the entire spectacle of the trial, from the opening to the closing statements, comprehending and evaluating all the evidence and testimony offered in between, in order to arrive at a single judgment concerning whether the defendant is guilty or not guilty of a crime. To do so, conflicting appearances must be sorted out. The truth must be thoughtfully discerned. Now, it might seem that the jury, unable to ask questions, is extraneous to the proceedings, but of course that's false. The entire courtroom drama plays out for the jury and no one else. In fact, the jury is even referred to as "the presence," and certain technical issues must be discussed while the jury is absent. Unlike the spectator to the baseball game, then, the jury is essential to the action. As a jury member, your sacred civic duty is to determine the truth as it arises in the murky appearances of the courtroom proceedings. So it is with phenomenology; your principal goal is to discern the truth of experience itself, to actualize the possibility of presence afforded by being the kind of beings we are, to arrive at not only the truth of this, that, or the other thing but the truth about truth itself and how it arises in our experience.

The Essentiality of Experience

Socrates raises eyebrows by asking a seemingly obvious question, "What is x?," and then showing that people who think they know the answer to the question in fact know nothing of the sort. So, to take one example, he asks, "What is justice?" Conventional wisdom says it is to tell the truth and pay one's debts. Socrates wonders, though, whether it is really just to return things owed to people when they are out of their mind; surely it is not just to return someone's car keys to a person that is drunk, for example. So there's something amiss about that as a definition for justice. What Socrates does is ask an obvious question and explode a conventional answer in order to ready the mind to inquire further into the true essence of a thing. Right there in the ordinary, right where we think we've got the answer handy, Socrates alerts us to our ignorance, alerts us that there something elusive, something slippery and strange, inside us. Socrates's question about essence becomes a permanent possession of the philosophical enterprise. He happens, long ago, upon something that belongs to us in the present. We today still ask after the essence of things if we think deeply at all.

Modern philosophy broke ranks with classical philosophy by shifting attention from the essence of things to the experience of things. Immanuel Kant, for example, turns our attention to the seemingly obvious question concerning how it is at all possible that we should be able to experience and thereby know things. He finds this puzzling because experience seems to be something incidental to things, something that could hardly provide the foundation of knowing how things must be, and yet it is only via experience that we know things. Kant happens upon a mode of experience that is not incidental but necessary and this mode is what enables knowledge. Now, it is hard to think of anything more present to us than ourselves and the world that is present to us, but here again in this obviousness, modern thought raises a scarlet question

Am I only always guessing?

mark, alerting us to how deeply puzzling it is that we are open in our being to things we are not. So unsettling is this question that it remains a permanent temptation to deny the terms of the question and to say that we are not open but instead closed, closed in upon our own representations and neural happenings, unable to do anything more than generate guess after guess concerning what might be found "out there," beyond the confines of our consciousness or the folds of our skin.

Phenomenology potently combines these two forces in philosophy, search for the elusive essence of things and wonder concerning the possibility of experiencing things. It renews Socrates's relentless inquiry into *what* things are.[10] It renews the modern relentless inquiry into *how* things are experienced.[11] Phenomenology's hybrid method holds these two counter movements in tension by applying them to each other. It asks, "*How* can we experience essences, and *what* is the essence of experience?" Now, could there be anything more obvious than what things are or how they are experienced? Yet it is right here that phenomenological philosophy awakens, calling to us, summoning us to inquiry, telling us that there is much honest searching we must do if we are to arrive where we think we are but are not—at the truth. Indeed, Husserl even makes bold to say that "philosophy may be paradoxically, but not unprofoundly, called the science of the trivial."[12] For a philosopher who wants wisdom this seems to

Phenomenology potently combines two forces in philosophy: search for the elusive essence of things and wonder concerning the possibility of experiencing things.

be a strange claim to make. Why think of philosophy as trained on the "trivial"? Because "it is precisely behind the obvious that the hardest problems lie hidden."[13] Phenomenology investigates two *seemingly* trivial but in fact profound topics: the experience of essences and the essence of experience. It thereby transcends the opposition of the ancients and the moderns and inaugurates a new era for philosophizing, one brimming with possibility.

Behold the Phenomena

Inspired by the modern world picture, which sees experience as a neural event, Friedrich Nietzsche becomes deeply suspicious of appearances: "A painter without hands who wished to express in song the picture before his mind would, by means of this substitution of spheres, still reveal more about the essence of things than does the empirical world."[14] The poverty of sensory stimulus gives us no means to access the reality of things. Despite this view, he becomes increasingly nostalgic for a richer sense of experience:

Oh, those Greeks! They knew how to live. What is required for that is to stop courageously at the surface, the fold, the skin, to adore appearance, to believe in forms, tones, words, in the whole Olympus of appearance. Those Greeks were superficial—*out of profundity*. And is not this precisely what we are again coming back to, we daredevils of the spirit who have climbed the highest and most dangerous peak of present thought and looked around from up there—we who have looked *down* from there? Are we not, precisely in this respect, Greeks? Adorers of forms, of tones, of words? And therefore—*artists*?[15]

Nietzsche pens these lines in 1886; confronting the same situation just fourteen years later, Husserl happens upon another possibility and could say: "Adorers of forms, of tones, of words? And therefore—*phenomenologists*?"

Here's Husserl's decisive innovation. We do not *confect* experience in the fashion of an artist; we *constitute* experience, thereby letting the things of experience show themselves as they are. "'*Constituting*,'" Heidegger writes, "does not mean producing in the sense of making and fabricating; it means *letting the entity be seen in its objectivity*."[16] We do have to do something to become receptive to what's there, but this activity does not compromise but rather enables the receptivity. After all, if we are to determine the population of Felicity, California, we have to do something, tally the number of residents, in order to know how many live there. But the counting activity does not *make* it true that Felicity has a population of two; the activity

We have to act. Something must act upon an activity. It is the acting that helps us see a reality & react to it.

lets us *register* the objective truth that there are only two people that live there.

To recover the truth of experience, we need to raise anew the question of the essence of experience. The chapters of this book unpack each of the following terms. Experience does not take place in our brains but in the public *world*. Perception is the achievement of our whole body as we explore the world; *flesh* names the way our experiential exploration is inscribed into the bearing of our bodily being, making our experiential exploration available to the experience of others. *Speech*, which is instituted in bodily presence, opens up a world of absence; we can talk to each other about things we don't presently perceive and in fact about things we may never perceive. *Truth* concerns the way our claims about things are confirmed by our experience so that the very things meant in their absence are present to experience just as they were meant; the intuited identity of presumed and experienced things yields a pregnant conception of truth. The *life* lived by us who are ordered through perception and speech to truth is a life that exceeds that of other animals. In the experiential register, *love* comes into its own as a way of seeing, of enabling the life of the beloved to be experienced as such. *Wonder* is the experience in which something erupts into the field of experience, upsetting the ordinary, and ushering in the extraordinary. These terms—world, flesh, speech, truth, life, love, and wonder—are bound up with one another in experience. Husserl writes, "We search, as it were, in zig-zag fashion, a metaphor all the more apt since the close interdependence of our various . . . concepts leads us back again and again to our original analyses, where the new confirms the old, and the old the new."[17] The phenomenological method is a manner of clarifying the modality of experience that is written into the very fabric of experience, of aggravating wonder to the point of having us confront experience as a whole. The phenomenological movement is the history of those who grapple with the logic of experience, those who open up for us this possibility of experiencing and thinking, this radical possibility for renewing human life together.

The phenomenological movement rallies itself with the motto, *To the things themselves*. Rather than resting content with theoretical reconstructions of experience that stand in between us and things, phenomenologists return to the experience *of things* in their truth. Heidegger writes,

> The phenomenological maxim "*to the things themselves*" is addressed against construction and free-floating questioning in traditional concepts which have become more and more groundless. That this maxim is self-evident, that it nevertheless has become necessary to make it into an explicit battle cry against free-floating thought, characterizes the very situation of philosophy.[18]

We must go back to the things themselves because in equating appearance with mere appearance we've tragically let ourselves lose contact with things. Phenomenology is a relatively new movement, but it is the explicit recovery of a possibility so old that it is resident right there in human experience. Scheler writes, "The phenomenological philosopher, thirsting for the lived-experience of being, will above all seek to drink at the very *sources* in which the contents of the world reveal themselves."[19] Phenomenology makes a fresh start by returning to philosophy's origin in experience.

WORLD

If you stand close enough to an impressionist painting—close enough to raise the ire of an overly attentive museum guard—the dazzling image dissolves into a play of lumpy colors. If you take a step back, the patterns again come into focus and there emerges a pond of lily pads or Rouen Cathedral resplendent with evening light. Though the painter Paul Cézanne valued the impressionist's palette of color, he thought they had missed something essential about perception—the thing. He therefore took to outlining the objects in his paintings with thick black lines. For this reason, the pears in his still life paintings pop off the table and his farmhouse juts out from the surrounding wilderness of foliage. Now who was right about perception, the impressionists or Cézanne? If you look at a pear on your table, you won't see it circumscribed by a black border. Instead, you'll see it as a locus of color bathed in light. In this way, it seems Cézanne misunderstood perception. Nonetheless, Cézanne's subjects always seem more tangible and therefore more real than the impressionist's alternatives. Why? While our experience does not involve an outline of objects, our experience does involve the thickness of things as they stand forth in the field of perception. A good way of expressing this thickness on a two-dimensional surface is to outline the object so that it appears to rise out from the canvas. Actual experience is four-dimensional, adding depth and movement through time. Look at a pear on a table. It appears as a circular surface of color only if we look at it with one eye closed or in a photo snapshot. With both eyes open and moving about it we see it as an orb, as something with more than one side. Pick it up, turn it over, remove the sticker, and take a bite. Cézanne's outlines show us the fact that experience is experience *of things*, and these things of experience have a solidity and substantiality corresponding to our bodily exploration of them.

Cézanne alerts us to the pedestrian but wonderful fact that a thing affords horizons of exploration. The side it shows, the angle it offers, is always but one of the sides to see, one of the angles to take in. There's a backside to the pear and an underside to the table. The price of presence is a corresponding absence. To see one side, the other must become hidden. To be inside means not to see the outside and vice versa. Husserl expresses the way a present side

Can we really take in all of a thing or experience at once?

Figure 1 Paul Cézanne, *Still Life with Apples and Pears*. The Metropolitan Museum of Art, New York, Bequest of Stephen C. Clark, 1960.

includes awareness of its absent sides as follows: "Only in this way can we understand how consciousness reaches out beyond what it actually experiences. It can so to say mean beyond itself, and its meaning can be fulfilled."[1] Presence points to absences that may yet be made present. In this way, perception always leads to further perception. Cézanne's paintings express something of the horizon of exploration, something of this play of presence and absence, that is at work in an experience. Merleau-Ponty writes that "Cézanne knows already what cubism will repeat: that

we must be aware of all we are not seeing / feeling who've experience something

the external form, the envelope, is secondary and derived, that it is not that which causes a thing to take form."[2] Perception is not simply the passivity of impressions; it is the activity of letting things show themselves as the very things they are. It involves what phenomenology calls *constitution*, the activity of letting the thing stand forth as the thing it is. Thanks to constitution, things emerge as they are from the backdrop of a wilderness of untamed impressions. In this way, Cézanne touches upon a fundamental discovery of phenomenology—intentionality.

Intentionality

The phenomenological structure of intentionality applies globally to all our experience. All experience is a matter of experiencing something *as* something, and all thought is a matter of targeting something *as* something. Experience and thoughts cannot be understood simply in terms of their "inward" aspect, for they are ineluctably "outward" as well, putting us into contact with a public world of things. The first time a child sees a pair of scissors, there is an experience of puzzlement. Here is something but it cannot be intended as what it is. But a parent or caregiver demonstrates by saying, "These are scissors," while displaying the cutting, snip, snip. For the rest of their lives, the children will be able to intend scissors as scissors.[3]

Whenever we experience or think, we experience or think *of* things. Not only do we engage them, we engage them under a particular aspect, *as* something or another. The phenomenological analysis of intentionality helps us to see that experience is mediated through language and other people in order to present to us, in various modalities, what is there to be experienced.

Every time we view a movie we modify intentionality. We see Anne Hathaway as *Les Misérables*'s "Fantine" rather than as *Alice in Wonderland*'s "White Queen" or *Ocean's 8*'s "Daphne Kluger," and we intend these characters differently than when we see Anne Hathaway as herself when she appears at the Oscars. How does one and the same person appear both as herself and as another? We intend her differently in both cases due to a shift in context. In the one she appears as part of a fictional world; in another she appears as transcending that world, as belonging to the world in which we can meet her in person. This can be humorously complicated and we can easily make sense of the complication. In *Ocean's 12*, Julia Roberts plays two characters. She plays a fictional character, Tess, who happens to look like the famous movie star, Julia Roberts, and she plays Julia Roberts, the famous movie star. Perceptually, the actress Julia Roberts looks the same in both instances, but the viewer, without any difficulty, intends one appearance of Julia Roberts as "Tess" and the other as "Julia Roberts." Everyone who sees the movie with understanding shares in the same public appearance. We have to do something to enable things to appear as they are but thanks to this activity things can appear as such for each of us together.

How do you intend to see ppl?

Are Tables in Our Heads?

Intentionality is often presented as the novel break-through of phenomenology, but this is misleading; everyone thinks thoughts are *of* things; the question concerns the status of these intended things. Are they in the head or out in the world? The phenomenological breakthrough concerns the publicness of appearances; they are not private things in our heads but public dimensions of things themselves. Appearances belong to the experiential world that each of us shares through our own resources.

Think of sitting down for a meal. If you sit at the head of the table and look at its rectangular top, it will appear trapezoidal. (Of course, you won't think the shape really *is* trapezoidal, only that its rectangularity must appear as trapezoidal from this perspective.) If you scoot your chair to the corner, the top will appear trapezial, a quadrilateral with no parallel sides. If you move to the side, it will again appear trapezoidal, but this time the base is long and the sides are short. Finally, toss to the side all manners and stand on top of the table, peering down. Then the rectangular table will no longer appear trapezoidally or trapezially but rectangularly. What are we to make of this play of appearances?

The modern philosopher David Hume thinks it is obvious that the play of appearances happens inside our heads. First, he acknowledges that it is commonsensical to believe that a table remains the table it is independent of our experience of it. But then he insists that philosophy *destroys* this belief by proving that all we ever experience are our own subjective impressions; we cannot access the things themselves:

[handwritten margin note: No matter the truth, you can only ever view it through you and/ed your eyes. The world will not react to my truth t, I to others]

> This very table, which we see white, and which we feel hard, is believed to exist, independent of our perception, and to be something external to our mind, which perceives it. Our presence bestows not being on it: our absence does not annihilate it. It preserves its existence uniform and entire, independent of the situation of intelligent beings, who perceive or contemplate it.
>
> But this universal and primary opinion of all men is soon destroyed by the slightest philosophy, which teaches us, that nothing can ever be present to the mind but an image or perception, and that the senses are only the inlets, through which these images are conveyed, without being able to produce any immediate intercourse between the mind and the object.[4]

Why might philosophy lay waste to common sense? He reasons as follows: "The table, which we see, seems to diminish, as we remove farther from it: but the real table, which exists independent of us, suffers no alteration: it was, therefore, nothing but its image, which was present to the mind."[5] So here are his two propositions and its apparent conclusion:

1. The perception of the table constantly changes.

2. The real table does not.

3. Therefore, we perceive something else—mental images—not the real table.

Hume thinks the third proposition is inescapable. "These are the obvious dictates of reason; and no man, who reflects, ever doubted, that the existences, which we consider, when we say, this house and that tree, are nothing but perceptions in the mind, and fleeting copies or representations of other existences, which remain uniform and independent."[6] The table *is* rectangular and not trapezoidal or trapezial; the latter must be something purely mental. Is life all about angels?

How can phenomenology upset this line of reasoning to restore access to the things themselves? How can it side with commonsense and premodern philosophers such as Aristotle and Augustine against "the obvious dictates of

Point of view	Aspect	Shape
From the head	Trapezoid	Rectangular
From a corner	Trapezium	Rectangular
From a side	Trapezoid	Rectangular
From above	Rectangle	Rectangular

Figure 2 Perceiving a table.

reason"? Husserl agrees with Hume's first two propositions, and he even gives a more acute analysis of the first,
the table's ever-changing perception. Not only does the appearance of the table change when we walk around it but
even when we remain motionless the perception changes
from moment to moment due to the "constant flow" of
time: "I close my eyes. My other senses are not in any relation to the table. Now I have no perception of it. I open
my eyes and I have the perception again. *The* perception?
Let us be more precise. Recurring, it is under no circum-
stances individually the same. Only the table is the same,
and I am conscious of it as identical in the synthetic consciousness that joins the new perception with memory."[7]
Husserl agrees with Hume that the table itself is unchanging. How can he stave off Hume's inevitable conclusion
that we experience not the things themselves but instead
private impressions? Husserl advances a different third
proposition:

1. The perception of the table constantly changes.

2. The real table does not.

3. The changing perception presents the same real table
in all its reality. I think therefore I am. I perceive
therefore it is.

Husserl offers this real self-sameness not as an abstract
thesis but as something continually and inescapably

confirmed by experience. How might this be? Hume juxtaposed changing and unchanging from an abstract point of view and found them incompatible. Husserl enters concretely into the contours of experience and finds changing and unchanging necessarily entwined. Experience itself, thoughtfully enacted, refutes Hume and confirms Husserl:

> One and the same shape (given in person *as* the same) appears continuously again and again "in a different way," in adumbrations of shape that are always different.[8]

Husserl calls these various appearances *adumbrations*, or so many shadows the thing itself casts as it is explored by us. The thing does not hide behind its appearances. The appearances rather are the thing's disclosure. We experience a rectangular table as rectangular only by its appearing trapezoidal while sitting next to it or trapezial while sitting at a corner. The trapezoidal or trapezial appearance is what gives us the rectangularity of the table. Husserl saves the publicness of the table by distinguishing—though not separating—appearances, on the one hand, and that which shows up thanks to appearances, on the other. Appearances are indeed fleeting, as Hume suggests, but they constantly present the reality of the perceived thing. Hence, appearances are not simply private, for they put us into contact with the public features of things.

How we perceive something is how we actually interact with the reality of that thing.

Husserl sees two dimensions to the appearances of a thing. First, there's the spatiality of it. Sit in one and the same seat viewing the table from the same vantage point; the table will look the same. In fact, you and I could switch seats and, provided we're the same height, it would look exactly the same to both of us. This look, which each of us can share, is the shape of the thing as seen from here, as correlated with a particular vantage point. But there's also the temporality of it. Sit in one and the same seat viewing the table from the same vantage point. Close your eyes and then look again. The perception has now been interrupted and resumed. It is not identically the same perception even though it presents the same aspect as before. This unrepeatable, temporally individuated appearance is an adumbration. Thanks to the private dimension of experience, how it looks now from here, we can together access how it looks at any time from here or there, which is to say, we can together access how it is. The interplay of different points of view gives us purchase on the thickness of things; they are not what they are just for each of us alone but for each of us together. Husserl writes that "it has never been recognized that the otherness of 'someone else' becomes extended to the whole world, as its 'Objectivity,' giving it this sense in the first place."[9] Hume dissolves appearances into private mental impressions; Husserl restores appearances into public displays of things.

Our perceptions mingle. They can help us get a deeper understanding of a truth we cannot really get on our own.

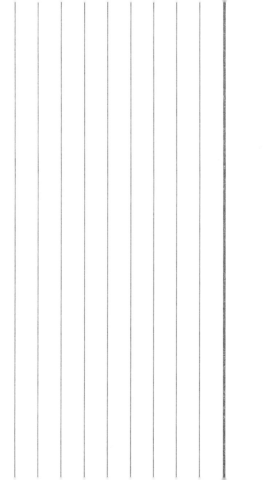

Philosophers like Hume routinely mistake perception to be a kind of picturing, and they accordingly locate the pictures in our heads, thereby giving rise to the problem of how these pictures relate to the otherwise unknown somethings they depict. In reality, appearances bond us to what appears rather than stand between us and what appears; they belong to the very being of the thing that appears.

In this way, Husserl never tires of saying that perception presents something in the flesh. "The perception of a thing does not, as though it were a memory or phantasy, re-present something not present; it attends to what is present, it apprehends something itself, as it is bodily present."[10]

Aren't Appearances in the Brain?

Sensory stimuli seem to be nothing more than "raw data."[11] Appearances consequently have to happen in the way the brain works up that data into a model. Nietzsche, for example, regards all words as metaphors for images that are themselves metaphors for nerve stimuli, and he further thinks there is no way for us to know how these metaphors map onto anything outside our heads.[12] Searle writes similarly:

In reality, appearances bond us to what appears rather than stand between us and what appears; they belong to the very being of the thing that appears.

> My basic assumption is simply this: . . . The brain is
> all we have for the purpose of representing the world
> to ourselves and everything we can use must be
> inside the brain. Each of our beliefs must be possible
> for a being who is a brain in a vat because *each of us
> is precisely a brain in a vat*; the vat is a skull and the
> "messages" coming in are coming in by way of impacts
> on the nervous system.[13]

The phenomenologist Robert Sokolowski argues, by contrast, that sense perception is not a matter of brute im-
pacts on our sensory receptors. Rather, the energy that
our senses tap into is *ambient energy*: the light scattered by
a perceptible thing is a light configured by the very shape
and texture of a thing. Configured energy bears the appearance of a thing, the way it looks. In this way it differs
from radiant energy, which comes directly from its source
and accordingly bears no appearance.[14]

To appreciate the difference between ambient and
radiant energy, consider a prosaic example: you are driving home on a dark country road when your headlights
illumine a pair of eyes; you slam on the brakes and come
to a halt before a herd of wandering cattle. Compare the
cow's experience with your own. The cow was blinded by
the headlights, because the light came directly from its
source and did not reflect off any surfaces. By contrast, the
light did not blind you but instead gave you sight, because

the energy emitted by the headlights did not directly impact your sensory receptors but instead took a detour by reflecting off the cow itself, and in being reflected it was altered by the reflection; therefore, it could give you at a distance the look and shape of a cow's eyes and not an open road. Energy need not be a blunt impact that blinds; energy can mediate a manifestation.

How should we think of the brain and nervous system in light of the fact that ambient energy conveys appearances to us? Sokolowski suggests that the brain and nervous system can be thought of as similar to an ordinary glass lens that you can either look *through* or look *at*: it can be the transparent means for us to allow the world to be present to us; it can also be something that we make into an object in its own right, noting its physical properties.[15] You need your brain to receive the energy of the cow's appearance, but the appearance is not the brain and neither are you. And you are able to see the cow thanks to the light, thanks to your brain, but not in such a way that the light or your brain stands in between you and the cow. The cow appears thanks to this transparently functioning means of transmitting the appearance, in the way you might see the cow through a pair of glasses or indeed the clear windshield.

Where are you in experience? You are not still another domino in the series: light, cow, configured energy, rods and cones, nerve stimuli, brain, *you*. You are rather the enfleshed driver of the car who sees the cow. The physiology functions as a background condition for your experience, but not in such a way that you are derivable from or identical to that background. We crave a picture injecting ourselves into the process; we want to see ourselves layered on top of the biology, as yet another cog in the machine. But in fact the problem with the picture is that it leaves out precisely what we want pictured, the presence of a point of view. The simple truth is that the only way to conceive of a point of view is to occupy one.

When the brain and nervous system are in operation, they give us a world of things. Only when we ignore our own operative point of view can it seem—to whom? one wonders—that the brain and nervous system are opaque obstacles to the world of things. In identifying us with our brains, Searle makes Hume's mistake; he privatizes appearances and migrates them indoors, into the folds of our gray matter. In doing so, he implicitly isolates us from each other and from a joint world of truth. By contrast, phenomenologists recover the publicness of appearances; in doing so, they likewise demonstrate that experience takes place not in our skulls but instead out there with others among things. The experiential body opens a field of presence and absence in which language can arise and give voice to truth.

We are our brains but even more than that, we are all the stimuli we take in. Even if we only see a shadow that shadow informs & shapes us, and we can see the same shadow. We can come the same ground we

the shape & form a shared or at least understandable truth

The simple truth is that the only way to conceive of a point of view is to occupy one.

World as Place of Presence

Heidegger gives his signature example of a hammer that we use to get a job done. We start thinking about the hammer instead of the job only if the hammer turns up missing or if it breaks. Only if the hammer loses its inconspicuousness can we look at it as a thing and investigate its physical properties.[16] Ordinarily, we understand it by taking it in hand and hammering. What is at work in such examples of everyday things? The point of these phenomenological exercises is not to suggest that practicality is the essence of things or that we should be pragmatists in our self-understanding. Indeed, Heidegger writes, "It never occurred to me . . . to try and claim or prove with this interpretation that the essence of man consists in the fact that he knows how to handle knives and forks or use the tram."[17] After all, there are also experiences that transcend the practical, such as the experience of beauty and the wonder before nature. Phenomenology offers accounts of the modalities of our experience of everyday things in order to illumine three points.

1. The things that occupy us do so in light of our overall interests. Consider a morning breakfast routine. My desire to secure food for myself and my loved ones, a desire anchored in the care I exercise over my own life, grounds this chain of meaning. I choose to alleviate hunger by serving toast, and that implicates me in a pattern

of actions: retrieving slices of bread, placing them in the toaster, waiting for them to get toasted, placing them on a plate, using a knife to cover them with jam and butter. These things—loaf, toaster, plate, knife, jam, butter, and so on—are entwined with one another; they take on the meaning that they have in light of my desire for toast, a desire that expresses the care I have for myself and my loved ones. Thus, what phenomenologists would like to call attention to with examples of tools and everyday routines is the way in which the things of the world have the meaning that they do in light of a web of significance that unfolds in reference to ourselves and our agency. Experience does not involve a solitary self over and against an isolated thing. Experience involves us navigating a rich context of things together with others.

2. The things that occupy our attention do so by means of the interplay of presence and absence. We might place a piece of bread in the toaster oven, get the coffee brewing, and pour a glass of orange juice. As we do these things, our attention might range from the ache in our neck to the lack of tidiness on the counter or might leap ahead to the projects due later in the day. Ordinarily, our attention does not rest on the items comprising the breakfast routine—the bread, toaster, coffee grounds, glass, and orange juice. Rather, they are in the background while we attend to other matters. However, it is possible for these items to become conspicuous and to emerge from the

background into the foreground. It is possible for these items to become present in a heightened fashion. For example, suppose the toast comes out burned to a crisp. Our thoughts will come back from planning the day and rest with this present item. Why, we'll wonder, did the toast not get browned but instead blackened? Ah, we'll discover, the setting was off, the tray too low or what have you. We'll fix the problem and then return to our thoughts about distant things while our routine resumes.

3. The play of presence and absence happens thanks to what phenomenologists call world. Not only do we deal with things in the field of presence; at any moment, each of us can shift attention from things, whether present or absent, to presence and absence itself. When we do so, we do not leave behind things but we now think of them as other than the field of presence and absence itself. The movement of the past and future of time and the near and far of space happens here in this place of openness. The world in this sense is *not* the globe or the Earth viewed by zooming out in Google Maps. The world in this sense is *not* some collection of things, the set of everything that is. It is, rather, a realm of possible experience, the site in which we encounter things that we are not. To be human means to be those beings that dwell in this shared world of experience thanks to which we can meet with particular things.

The various presences and absences of things in our experience happen against the backdrop of presence and

To be human is to
be open to experience
on the end of?

absence itself. Heidegger writes, "It is utterly unthinkable how something, a natural thing, could be encountered in its pure bodily presence, if not on the basis of the *prior presence of world*."[18] Accordingly, if humans are defined by experience, they are defined by what Heidegger calls being-in-the-world.

Cézanne suggests the play of presence and absence in perception by outlining his objects; the cubists do so by playfully making present all the absent sides at once. In this way they come up with an alternate way of calling attention to the thickness of four-dimensional experience while being similarly bound to two-dimensional space. Yet the cubists do not pull us into experience as Cézanne does; they do not capture the invitation inscribed into appearance. Instead, cubists rebuff us from the field of experience; in their paintings, perception has already happened; it's all splayed out; there's nothing hidden for us to discover. Phenomenology, like Cézanne, leads us inside an experience that is underway and awakens us to the wonder of wonders that beings appear to us and invite our continuous exploration. Husserl writes,

> Phenomenological explication does nothing but *explicate the sense this world has for us all, prior to any philosophizing*, and obviously gets solely from our experience—*a sense which philosophy can uncover but never alter*, and which, because of an essential

necessity, not because of our weakness, entails (in the case of any actual experience) horizons that need fundamental clarification.[19]

While experience invites us to make sense of things, phenomenology invites us to make sense of the world in which such experience occurs.

FLESH

Suppose you look in a mirror. Do you see yourself, or a reflection? It seems it cannot be yourself, since you are here seeing so you could not also be over there being seen. Yet the reflection presents you as though you were not only here but also over there. Merleau-Ponty observes, "The mirror itself is the instrument of a universal magic that changes . . . myself into another, and another into myself."[1] Just as you can look at a picture and see yourself in another place, so you can look in a mirror and see yourself elsewhere even while you remain where you are. The difference is that the mirror image does not lag behind you in the past but is a live image in real time. Now suppose you were to look away from the mirror and down at your hand holding a toothbrush. You wouldn't see a reflection of your hand over there but your hand right where it is. Suppose further you used your other hand to touch this

Just as you can look at a picture and see yourself in another place, so you can look in a mirror and see yourself elsewhere even while you remain where you are.

toothbrush-holding hand. That hand would then be touching the toothbrush and being touched itself; that hand would be feeling and felt.

Phenomenologists use the term *flesh* to speak of the twofold experiential body, which both gives us a world of perceived things and makes us one of the very things able to be perceived. As a gift to its language, the German tongue has two words for the body, *Leib* and *Körper*. One names a living, experiencing, and expressive body, and the other an inert physical thing. It is a shortcoming of the English language that we don't have the same distinction, and we accordingly must call both living and nonliving bodies "bodies." What comes closest to *Leib*, the living body, is the English word *flesh*, a word that is deeply evocative, suggesting something visceral or carnal. In other contexts, I prefer to call this sense the "animate body," but here, in an effort to express phenomenology in English rather than mere Latinate or Germanic expressions, I prefer "flesh." Note that I use it in a technical way to name the living body that experiences the world; I am not emphasizing its associations with the sensual appetite. Flesh is the living body, which both feels and can be felt, both sees and can be seen. As we experience the world, flesh advertises to others our experiential engagement with things. By opening the world for us and for each other together, it readies us to speak about things and register them in their truth.

Present in the Flesh

Pick up a stone in your hand. It's cold and smooth. Turn it over, grasp it. Note how it feels good to finger its rounded contours. Plunge it in water; feel the coolness of the water on your hand but also see how the wetness brings out vividly the stone's natural coloration; the light plays so beautifully off the glossy finish. Your own flesh allows this lifeless thing to be made manifest as it is. Now run your hand through the thick tufts of a dog's coat. Feel her frame heave with every breath and subtly respond to every stroke; note the rush of comforting warmth that wells up in you; get knocked over as she, moved by your affection, nuzzles you and tries to lick your face. Flesh opens us to explore the world and meet with not only things but also fellow explorers of things.

The experiential play of presence and absence, examined in chapter 2, requires something more to be understood. Presence is always presence *to* someone. "Let me see it," we say, and of course we really want to hold it, to turn it over, and have it present to us. We want to make it present by bringing it close to us. And that means presence requires the flesh. When we bring something close, it is not a matter of having it physically next to us; it is a matter of having it near us so that we can profitably explore it, examine it, and thereby come to know it. In this way, experience is not something that happens *in me*. It is something that happens *in the world* through the active exploration accomplished by my flesh.

Imagine arriving in a country in which everyone speaks only an unknown language. Now imagine something stranger still: you don't know English or any other language whatsoever but are completely bereft of speech. How could you come to learn to speak the language spoken by those around you? You cannot ask what something is called, and you cannot, as it were, attempt to pair your English thoughts with the unknown word-sounds you're overhearing. You'd have to start from scratch. What would you have to go on? The situation might seem impossible—positively hopeless—except for the fact that each one of us has found ourselves in just such a situation and somehow coped successfully so that we now have a sure command of our mother tongue. English, French, Chinese, or any other language we might know consists of a system of signs that mean what they do thanks to convention. We do not come hardwired knowing the meaning of any words but instead must somehow decode them. A foreign language can be learned in reference to our mother tongue, but how did we come to acquire our first language? How did that happen?

Psychologists point to something called "mind-reading" to explain the prelinguistic bridge from self to other.[2] Infants read the minds of those about them and thereby come to understand the meaning of overheard words: ball, cat, mom, and so on. Psychologists don't intend any magical faculty, a kind of sixth sense that gives us a conduit to the hidden thoughts of others. Instead, they mean that outward behavior occasions inferences to hidden mental states. The language user might point to an item while saying "ball" and the infant can thus infer that the bodily bearing indicates the item from the world the word means. This appeal to mind-reading, however, does not quite fit the phenomenological facts. A careful attention to experience reveals that meaning does not lurk hidden behind the body but is instead made manifest in and through the movement of the body. That is, infants learn to speak not thanks to skills of inference but thanks to the natural manifestation of flesh.[3] The meaning is not hidden behind the body; the meaning is embodied in movement toward or away from items of interest. Infants learn speech thanks to "body-reading," not mind-reading.

Try this activity. Stand in the middle of a busy square and stare intently upward at something, a circling bird perhaps. Your gaze will be contagious, as others will spontaneously clue into your attention, which is made available thanks to your bodily behavior: "What is it? What do you see?" People will not have to infer that you are looking up earnestly; they'll see that. Of course, they won't know what you're looking at unless you tell them or they look to see for themselves. Ordinarily we attend to the embodied attentions of others without much thought. There we are outside the store spotting a rare Model A Ford or the Oscar Meyer hotdog car. We see not only the unusual vehicle; we see that others are seeing it too. Precisely because experience takes place in the world thanks to our flesh, our experience is not private but is available to those about us. Flesh places us in a world of present and absent things, and it places us in that world with others who can experience our flesh and thus experience our experience. Our living bodies give each of us a vantage point on the world, and, in doing so, they enable the vantage point of others to be experienced as well. In this way, flesh is a necessary corollary of the publicness of appearance that was examined in chapter 2. The primal language, prior to any and every conventional one, is the natural meaning of our flesh.

Flesh's Visibility

With security cameras in our private residences no less than public places, today more than ever we are keenly aware that we not only see but are seen. Besides important questions about privacy, our visibility touches upon a basic philosophical question: Just what do others see when they see us, and what do we see when we look upon others?

The father of modern philosophy, René Descartes, looked out of his window and wondered if the people passing by in the square below were not in fact robots wearing human clothes. He was in his right mind, but he wondered in a contemplative key how we might be absolutely sure of what we see when we think we see other people. After all, what do we see except external appearances? We don't, as it were, intuit their souls or conscious lives. He therefore came up with a test to distinguish robots from people. First, ask them a variety of complicated questions and monitor their replies; second, get them to perform a variety of complicated tasks. If they could do both competently, they must be creative rather than programmed; they must be human, not machine.[4] In this way, Descartes grapples with what might seem to be an important question: How can we be sure that what appears to be someone else is not rather something else in disguise? For those outside phenomenology, the so-called problem of other minds is unsolvable. It becomes so by regarding the world as populated by two kinds of things: subjects that can be experienced only from the inside and objects that can be experienced only from the outside. Here is an object in my subjective sensory field. What special concerns might motivate me to project into it something of my own subjectivity? Why should I attribute an inner life to *it*? What might assure me that my neighbor is not after all a robot or a metaphysical zombie?

One solution offered by philosophers is *analogical inference*. I know of my own experience from the inside. I see from the outside a body behaving in a certain way. I also see my own body from the outside behaving in a certain way. I reason that just as my inside is conjoined with an outside so another outside must be conjoined with another inside. The body, behaving in such a way, must be the outside of another inside, another person. But most philosophers are not satisfied with this analogy. First, it seems to presuppose the very thing it sets out to prove, namely, that we are dealing with another self. If we're not, then the behavior we see is not analogous to our own. Second, it assumes that my behavior and the behavior of another exist side-by-side to be compared. But in fact I don't pay attention to my own behavior most of the time although I do pay attention to the behavior of others. My behavior is felt from the inside and the other's is there on display. They cannot be directly compared. Third, analogical inference is too elaborate a process to be operative in children and other animals, but we know that children and other animals are aware of other minds. They must not be inferential geniuses for that to occur. Instead, some other operation must take place. Many philosophers therefore offer a different solution, called *reason to the best explanation*. As we look out at these bodies behaving purposively, it seems the best explanation for this behavior is that we're dealing with fellow people. But again it is hard to get excited about this as an explanation, let alone the best available. It seems to conjure away the problem or dismiss it; it doesn't settle the doubts that creep in. Many philosophers have therefore given up on the problem.

Phenomenologists agree that the problem is unsolvable but they disagree on the reason why. It is unsolvable because it is a pseudo-problem, something artificially generated, a species of the sort of inept framing of problems that phenomenology comes on to the scene to dismantle. The problem with this question is that it is mistaken concerning the phenomenological facts of the matter. The whole inner–outer divide is an artificial construct, and consequently the idea that "behavior" is purely outward is mistaken. Experience is not tethered to the first person; other people do not show up in the first place as objects; they show up as fellow people.

Phenomenology dispenses with the artificial question, "What reason might I have for attributing minds to these perhaps lifeless bodies in my perceptual field?" Instead, it asks, "How do we, you and I, together emerge in the field of experience?" This is one of those cases where the collaborative nature of phenomenology clearly emerges; by applying themselves sequentially to the same problem, phenomenologists slowly bring the logic of experience to a more complete expression.

Scheler is the first phenomenologist to confront Descartes head on. He argues that the idea that we have direct access to ourselves and indirect access to others is entirely mistaken; in fact, he believes that we have the same access to others as we do to ourselves: "Our claim is . . . everyone can apprehend the experience of his fellowmen *just as directly (or indirectly)* as he can his own."[5] Moreover, he makes the case that our openness to others is not merely a function of other people happening to be around us. He says that a Robinson Crusoe, who never had seen a single fellow human, would nevertheless experience the absence of other people in terms of the lack of fulfillment of certain social acts such as love. Heidegger, with Scheler, wants to emphasize that even when no one else is around, others remain inscribed into our experience of things. In this way, others are not secondary in our experience but primary. Heidegger says our mode of being is defined by, among other things, *being-with* others.[6] Even something as ordinary as strolling through a neighborhood continues to call people to mind as we notice the upkeep of a yard or the vehicle parked out front. Still to insist on a fundamental openness to others even as we explore things does not account for how another person is directly experienced.

Edith Stein, in her dissertation under Husserl, unravels *how* other people come to be experienced. It happens thanks to the movement of their bodies and the intelligibility of their willed actions, which we understand as mirroring our own. Their animate movement appears essentially different from mechanical movement. Stein gives the example of the difference between seeing a nail driven into a wall and seeing a hand pricked. Mechanically, they are the same movement; but in the case of the prick we see it as being painful: "The hand senses pain if stuck, and we see this."[7] Stein thinks such perception involves the spontaneous projection of our own lives into the perceived flesh. The perception of living movement establishes various fellow perceivers, points of view on the whole, whose flesh expresses their experience of things. Husserl picks up on this motif, and his famous *Cartesian Meditations* points to the pairing of one's own flesh and that of another. Each of us experiences our body as being *here* and the body of another as being *there*, and we understand the other's point of view as being the one we could take were we to move from here to there.[8] The pairing of my point of view and another's, then, takes place because I understand my own point of view as potentially other with respect to where it is now.

Merleau-Ponty classically states the intertwining of self and other as happening thanks to flesh, which enables self and other to be "two openings . . . which both belong to the same world."[9] The mirroring of self and other happens thanks to the fact that flesh incarnates our points of view in a shared world. "For us the body is much more than an instrument or a means; it is our expression in the world, the visible form of our intentions."[10] He presents the Scheler–Heideggerian *openness* and the Stein–Husserl *pairing* as two layers of the experience of others. We remain radically open to the presence of others, and they show up in our field of experience thanks to flesh. In this account, phenomenology rejoins the classical intuitions of Augustine and Aristotle against Descartes's alienation of self and other.

> A Cartesian does not see *himself* in the mirror; he sees a dummy, an "outside," which, he has every reason to believe, other people see in the very same way but which, no more for himself than for others, is not a body in the flesh. His "image" in the mirror is an effect of the mechanics of things. If he recognizes himself in it, if he thinks it "looks like him," it is his thought that weaves this connection. The mirror image is nothing that belongs to him.[11]

Phenomenology insists, by contrast, that the mirror reveals what others see—my self on display. Owing to life, the life of our living, animate flesh, we can easily accommodate the reversibility of different points of view on the whole. The other shows up not thanks to an act of reasoning such as inference but instead thanks to the perceived reversibility of flesh, which instantiates different perspectives.

Consider the scene depicted in Mary Cassatt's *Sleeping Baby*. The presence of the baby to the mother is palpable. These are not lifeless bodies juxtaposed in space; here is flesh that feels and is felt. Our own flesh attunes us to the

Figure 3 Mary Cassatt, *Sleeping Baby*, ca. 1910. Pastel on paper; overall: 25½ × 20½ in. Dallas Museum of Art, Munger Fund, 1952.38.M.

dynamism of the mother's experience; her flesh mirrors our own. We have the world thanks to flesh and in having the world we meet with the flesh of others who likewise have the world.

With this invocation of flesh, phenomenology reunites the human with the animal and recognizes the genuineness of the life led by other animals. Suppose on a walk through the woods you happen upon a family of four armadillos foraging for food. They scamper here and there, rooting about, looking for sustenance. Their movement to sate hunger reveals their experience of it as well as the perception of the critters that will be the means for its alleviation. Their movement reveals their perceptual experience. Our own flesh allows us to clue into not only the actions of fellow humans but the actions of fellow animals as well. These might be alien and strange, but they are alien and strange as different presentations of flesh. Peer into the glassy black eyes of an emu that looks intently at you. Though you cannot fathom its experience, you can be in touch with its having experience. The points of view of humans and other animals will prove to be wildly different, but they are accessible to one another to some degree thanks to the kinship of flesh.

SPEECH

At first blush, a word seems to be something physical: shapes of ink on the page, pixels gathered on the screen, or sound waves in the air. Words do involve physicality of some sort but that is but the outward cloak of the mystery of the word. Here is a word: I see it, read it; I hear it, understand it; and suddenly I am not here with the word but elsewhere taken there by the word. For example, consider the words, "Cook Islands." If you read or hear those words with understanding, you no longer dwell with the physical shapes or sounds of the words; you don't focus on the peculiar concave shape of the *C* or the peculiar double circle of the repeated vowels, *oo*. Instead, your thoughts are elsewhere, there in fact with the cluster of islands in the South Pacific. Your thoughts hover there in some sort of suspense. Focused on those islands you wonder what I might say about it. "The Cook Islands are a popular honeymoon destination for those who cannot afford Tahiti." Words are marvelous not because they are physical things; they are marvelous because they are self-effacing as physical things, conveying our thoughts to one another, such that we are not brought into the heads of one another, but we are carried out into the world with one another. Words hold this power of enabling us to share thoughts about things even when they are absent to our perception. My words can carry you to a place you've never visited before and your words can do the same for me.

Words are what they are by hiding themselves in favor of thoughts and the thoughts are what they are by hiding themselves in favor of the things thought about. And those things we can think about together encompass everything that is, whether present or absent, whether existing or not.

Words and Images

The Belgian surrealist painter René Magritte produced a painting of a pipe on which he wrote, "Ceci n'est pas une pipe," *This is not a pipe*. At first, the statement seems evidently false, for the painting clearly depicts a pipe and not an elephant, an airplane, or any other object. This is indeed a pipe. And yet Magritte is calling attention to the nature of any image; it presents something that it is not. So yes, indeed, the painting presents a pipe and not an elephant,

Figure 4   René Magritte, *The Treachery of Images (This Is Not a Pipe)*. © 2019 C. Herscovici/Artists Rights Society (ARS), New York.

an airplane, or any other object, but it remains other than what it presents. It serves as a window onto the thing but not as a duplicate of the thing. One cannot smoke the picture of a pipe or feed the picture of an elephant. The painting is a thing in its own right, a piece of canvas coated with overlapping layers of paint infused with pigment. The painting can be cut from the frame and stolen, but one has not thereby stolen a pipe or an elephant.

To make his point about pictures, Magritte must call upon the resources of another human power. He must not only paint, he must write. Magritte is able to express the point, *This is not a pipe*, because of the power of language to make and track distinctions. In this case, the word "is" can identify the ambiguity of each and every picture, which depicts what it is not. The painting does depict a pipe, so in that sense, it is a pipe. But a depiction as depiction remains other than what it depicts and so in this sense it is not a pipe. Language can help us track our movement as we toggle back and forth from that which is depicted to the depiction, from pipe to picture.

There is a second feature of language operative in the image. The word "pipe" harbors a remarkable power. Though it appears to perception alongside the depicted pipe, the one that falls short of the original pipe you can smoke, these four letters, p-i-p-e, mere globs of paint, present a sound, pīp, that becomes infused with a directness to the pipe as a whole in its reality. Unlike the picture of a pipe, the word "pipe" reaches out to the thing itself. Hence, Magritte juxtaposes the power of images and the power of words and invites us to see that the word reaches out to the thing while the image falls short. The poverty of words, the fact that they direct us to an object without presenting that same object, turns out to be their great asset; they outstrip every image, every partial view that is given to experience, whether through images or even through perception. The word targets the thing itself.

Magritte's painting makes clear that the word goes beyond the image, but it is also true that the word goes beyond every perception too. For let us take out our pipe and lay it on our desk. Now we can write on a label *This is a pipe* and be right to see it as a true characterization of the item on our desktop. The perception gives what the image does not; the perception puts before us the real pipe, the one you can stuff with tobacco, light, and smoke. This is all true. But note this residual limitation. As I look at the pipe, I see it from only one side at a time; I can pick it up and turn it over, thereby disclosing the absent side, but I do so only by eclipsing the heretofore present side, casting it again into absence. Or again, I can look at its outside while its inside remains hidden, or I can peer into its bowl while casting the rest of it into absence. Perception of anything always involves a continual play of presence and absence. Again, Husserl calls these partial views "adumbrations," or so many shadows cast by our engagement with a thing. The perceptual object is never and can never be given from all angles and sides at once. Note, however, that because the word does not give the object, it can target the object as a whole. "Pipe" orients us to the pipe in its totality, not just as seen from here or there, filled or unfilled, smoked or unsmoked, turned over or let be. This feature of words has a further consequence. Though as a speaker of English I've said the word many times and though over the course of history other English speakers have said it countless times, there is but one single word, "pipe," and it refers to one and the same thing in all of these instances (setting aside other uses, such as pipes to carry water or pipes to play music). To paraphrase Husserl, the word *pipe* occurs only once in the English language.[1] Every painting of a pipe gives us something somewhat different, a new perspective on the thing; every instance of the word "pipe" for smoking is identical in its reference. In this sense, the word presents an ideal object.

Here's what we've got so far. A *word* is a sound infused with meaning that directs our thoughts to the thing meant; it targets an infinitely repeatable ideality. A *picture* or *image* is something that presents a thing from one side and vantage point while remaining other than the thing presented. A *perception* presents the thing itself but always via only one of the many possible angles and points of view. We've started in this simple way to alert us to the interplay of speech and perception. The decisive insight of phenomenology concerns the experiential character of speech and the linguistic character of experience.

From Presence to Absence

Let's suppose you and I are conversing. I say something about widgets. You ask what a widget is. I could point to a couple I have on hand. Or I can say it is "a small generic manufactured item." You are able to fix the referent to widgets thanks to this definition, thanks, in other words, to the fact that you already know what "small," "generic," "manufactured," and "item" happen to mean. Of course, if you didn't know the meaning of these words, I could likewise define them in terms of still other words. But for a definition to work, I'd have to arrive finally at some words that you already know, some words you don't need defined. Where does the initial stock of words come from, those that aren't known by definition?

As chapter 3 showed, initial words come from joint presence. The child taps into speech originally by cluing in to the way language users speak about the things around them, especially those things that are endlessly fascinating, such as balls, dogs, diggers, milk, and mom and dad. Infants hear a stream of speech and are able—thanks to the way flesh enables us to achieve joint presence—to pair speech and things.[2] The infant constantly overhears speech about all sorts of things: the plumber, a boss, the weather, and so on. At first the infant is able to pair words and things only when present things are talked about and when bodily movement makes these same things present in their presence: "Have you seen the little red ball?" "Sure. It's right here"—said as the speaker moves and fetches the ball.

Once we've begun to share words with others thanks to joint presence, it then becomes possible for us to reach out beyond joint presence to talk about all sorts of absent things. Speech originates in joint presence but soon leaves it behind. The child learns to ask what something is and to pay attention to linguistic context, and these new abilities to determine meaning open up the possibility of acquiring words for absent things. We can talk about the distant past, Caesar's exploits in Gaul; we can talk about the future, when humans populate another planet; we can talk about the abstract, electoral colleges and securities; we can talk about the imaginary, unicorns, the unknown, aliens, and the extinct, dodo birds. We can talk about what we had for breakfast and what we might have for dinner. Speech ranges out to encompass not only all that is, but all that has been, all that might be, and all that is merely fantastic.

Remarkably, even the above absences opened up by speech happen thanks to the inconspicuous presence of words. To hear the world-sound is to have the sound itself retreat in favor of whatever it means. Merleau-Ponty says, "The wonder of language is that it makes itself be forgotten: my gaze is drawn along the lines on the paper, from the moment that I am struck by what they signify, I no longer see them."[3] Simply repeat a word sound over and over, and it quickly becomes uncanny and strange: roof, roof, roof. The meaning becomes put out of play and the sound itself emerges unclothed. Normally, however, we hear the word-sound clothed in meaning, and it hides in favor of that which it points out—*roof*. We think of the coverings of buildings, things real enough to rebuff strong winds, torrential rain, and the force of winter storms. The present word-sound hides itself to direct us toward something that need not be present—roofs.

Grades of Presence

Phenomenology works out the various grades of presence, grades that are made possible thanks to the interweaving of speech and experience.

First, I can hear talk about a horse in passing. In Shakespeare's *Richard III*, the king calls out on the field of battle, "A horse! a horse! my kingdom for a horse!" Since I know the meaning of the word I can understand what he means without further ado. I don't have to imagine a horse or see a horse to be able to know what he wants. This last point is controversial, but consider the fact that while you read Shakespeare's play the Bard may mention a horse but also a whole host of figures engaged on the field of battle; as a matter of fact, you cannot nor do you need to imagine each individual object he mentions; speech happens fast and we imagine some things but we don't have to in order to follow someone's meaning. So we don't have to imagine something or see it in order to understand, but, nonetheless, such understanding, as Husserl puts it, "craves" sight.[4] Meaning functions in the absence of experience, whether perceptual or imaginary, but it nonetheless finds fulfillment in experience.

Second, I can imagine a horse. Shakespeare begins *Henry V* by pointing out the poverty of the stage compared with the realities depicted, and he bids his audience to use their imaginations to fill in the details: "Think when we talk of horses, that you see them / Printing their proud hoofs i' the receiving earth." I might imagine the erect frame, the muscular definition, the gleaming mane, the gallop, the neigh. Imagination provides partial grades of givenness but it doesn't quite give us the object itself.

Third, I might see a horse. Here I not only think about a horse, but I have it directly before me as it presents itself to me. The very thing meant by the word is given in the flesh. Heidegger says, "Intuition in the phenomenological sense implies no special capacity, no exceptional way of transposing oneself into otherwise closed domains and depths of the world."[5] Instead, to perceive the thing is to achieve "apprehension of what is itself bodily found just as it shows itself."[6] The presence of a thing is what it is against the possibility of its being merely meant or imagined.

Language and Experience

One of the peculiar things about philosophy is how it taps into ordinary powers that lie hidden in everyday speech.

The little word "as," for example, is central to phenomenology because it is central to experience. Look at something. What do you see? Socks, a dog, another person. You don't see some generic sensible thing; rather, you see what you see *as* something or another: *as* being socks, *as* being a dog, *as* being another person, and so on. Listen. What do you hear? A car passing, birds chirping, music playing. You don't hear raw noise that you subsequently interpret; you hear sounds *as* sounds of things; a sound you cannot identify as something or another attracts notice and you wonder, What was *that*? You don't know what to interpret it as. The *as* names the primary synthetic quality of experience that registers the identity of what is sensed and what is understood, of what is experienced and what can be said.

"It's a muggy day." Here we perceive the day *as* muggy; perhaps the humidity is high, the breeze nonexistent, and the temperature immoderate. We see all these things as together comprising the mugginess of a muggy day. Speech allows us to express the *as* of experience according to the *is* of speech. Taking the day *as* muggy enables us to express the fact that the day *is* muggy.

Typically, language and experience work in tandem. It's hard for us to experience what has not already been put into words, and it is hard to express an experience for the first time. The poet is one practiced in the extraordinary art of expanding the circle of language and experience.[7] Gerard Manley Hopkins, for example, looks out at the same world we see but invites us to understand it anew, to see it as manifesting what he calls "pied beauty." The first stanza of his poem by that name reads as follows:

Glory be to God for dappled things—

For skies of couple-colour as a brinded cow;

For rose-moles all in stipple upon trout that swim;

Fresh-firecoal chestnut-falls; finches' wings;

Landscape plotted and pieced—fold, fallow, and plough;

And áll trádes, their gear and tackle and trim.[8]

Hopkins invites us to see the sky, a cow, trout, finches, landscapes, and tools *as* manifestations of a single phenomenon, piedness. Further, he wants us to see piedness *as* something beautiful. Hopkins calls attention to the beauty of complex contrasts, something that shows up naturally enough in our experience, but something that it nevertheless takes a poet to highlight and name. As a result of his poetry, the beauty of what is "counter, original, spare, strange" can now show up for us more readily and explicitly when we look at things. Thereafter we can look out an airplane window at a patchwork of fields down below and register them as being beautiful in their piedness.

That is, thanks to Hopkins we can now better see things *as* instances of piedness and see piedness *as* something that is beautiful. Poets give us words to see something in a new way; they unlock a further *as* latent in the world of experience. In doing so they make available to the rest of us a richer way of understanding and speaking about experience.

Showing Things as They Are

Children under the age of two and primates who have learned sign language serially arrange their words one after another. They have semantics but no syntax. When syntax kicks in, children stop talking about the world by listing words in the way one might slide beads across a string. They start articulating the relations at work in the world that they experience in the way one might build a tower out of blocks. Syntax allows us to articulate the structures inherent in experience itself.[9] It elevates a synthesis in experience (an "as") into the synthesis of a sentence (an "is").

The sentence "In 1947, the Norwegian Thor Heyerdahl drifted from Peru to Polynesia on a balsa wood raft" involves a concatenation of syntactical relations. The sentence introduces not only terms but relations among them. Did he really *drift* across the Pacific? Was it really *on a balsa wood raft*? These syntactical relations raise questions that involve experience for confirmation. Not only the individual terms but the interweaving of the terms can be experienced: one might have been one of the five companions on the raft with him, the thousands receiving radio and newspaper reports of the journey, the scores watching the subsequent documentary, or the many viewing the recent cinematographic dramatization of the real-life story. In these cases, not only the semantic features, *Thor*, *drift*, *Peru*, *Polynesia*, *balsa wood*, *raft*, but also the syntactical interconnection *Thor drifted*, *from to*, *on*, can likewise be experienced in various degrees. What does phenomenology contribute to our understanding of the human discovery of syntax?

Phenomenology wishes to make explicit the wonderful, life-giving relation of language and experience. In the *Logical Investigations*, Husserl analyzes something mundane and seemingly humdrum, namely, how we might speak of a group of blackbirds flying away from our backyard.[10] In doing so, he is interested not in blackbirds but instead in the way in which events or states of affairs can be brought to linguistic expression. What astonishes him is that one and the same witnessed event can be expressed in many different ways, all of which correspond with the same state of affairs: "The blackbirds are flying away." "The group of birds are taking flight." "Those creatures with wings are now using them." "The yard is becoming depopulated with birds." "Those are black." Husserl wants us to notice several important points:

1. Language not only allows us to articulate experience; it allows us to articulate it in a variety of different ways. These ways are not necessarily synonymous; they are not in the examples above. Language gives us a freedom to organize and constitute a state of affairs depending on our interest and purposes. When we carve up the scene, we are both free to be creative and bound to be responsive to what's there.

We are at liberty to say any number of things, each of which will bring out different dimensions of the complex organization at work in the field of experience unfolding before us.

2. Despite this independence of the speech and the experienced event, it is nonetheless the case that the experienced event can confirm what is said. Whether I say, "The blackbirds are flying away" or "Those are black," looking out and seeing the avian exodus fulfills the meaning of the words. The very thing said is exhibited by the very experience of what's taking place. Language is somewhat independent of experience but can find in experience its confirmation.

3. Experience confirms not only the semantics of the sentence; it confirms the syntactical or categorial relations as well. This constitutes an insight of great importance. It is not the case, as modern philosophers from Descartes to

Nietzsche think, that experience consists only of isolated sensible properties and that all organization happens internally. It is rather the case, as classical and medieval philosophers from Aristotle to Aquinas knew, that experience consists also of relations among properties that can be externally registered. That is, when I look out I don't just experience isolated sensible qualities—black, avian shape, movement—rather, I look out and see not only the qualities but the *relations* that obtain among them. I see, I experience, I have given to me, the *complex* bird-taking-flight. Husserl says precisely because language finds confirmation in experience, experience has to be "widened" over what he calls the "categorial" domain.[11] This means that experience really does reach out to include not only sensible properties but the relations that happen among them. Phenomenology wants us to appreciate *how much* is given in experience—not just qualities but a whole rich texture of relations, a texture that language can articulate in a startling variety of ways.

It could seem that each of us goes about the world of experience growing in understanding of things. If we wish to clue someone in to what we are thinking, we must translate or express those thoughts into words. On this view, language works independent of experience and comes in only when we wish to communicate thoughts to others. The phenomenological movement provocatively returns language to experience in such a way that it

Phenomenology wants us to appreciate *how much* is given in experience—not just qualities but a whole rich texture of relations, a texture that language can articulate in a startling variety of ways.

regards the thing spoken about as "clothed" with the word; speech lets things appear as they are.[12] Heidegger writes, "Is not speaking, in what is most proper to it, a saying, a manifold showing of that which hearing, i.e., an obedient heeding of what appears, lets be said?"[13] To speak is to express the thoughts that arise by means of carefully attending to what appears. The speech of others constitutes so many invitations to look and see what there is to be seen, so many invitations to enrich one's own experience of things. In this way, speech frees us up to relate to absent things; language arises as the specific appropriation of a complex state of affairs; and all that can be said can be confirmed via some modality of experience.

TRUTH

One of the peculiar things about human beings is how much they delight in simple pleasures such as sinking a shot and getting nothing but net. It feels great to nail it, and it's also wonderful to see someone else make such a shot; there's something glorious about the achievement. Inversely, to miss the shot, to have it bounce off the rim or, worse, miss the rim entirely, brings about frustration and embarrassment. The feeling is attached to the achievement and the failure, so that not only the shooter but also the fan can enjoy one and the same success or bemoan one and the same misfire. When we hit the goal we feel an exhilarating sense of freedom, of fulfillment, and when we miss we feel confined, stifled. The freedom here is peculiar; it's the sense of freedom that comes in exercising a power. Think of the quintessential American experience of driving a car down the open road, and compare that with the experience of navigating city traffic. Most human activities have this same structure: we have a goal, delight in obtaining it, and become frustrated when we don't obtain it. You make a meal, you want it to turn out well; you raise kids, you want them to turn out well; you repaint your bathroom, you want it to turn out well. The burned meal, the unsuccessful child, the jarring color scheme are sources of embarrassment to varying degrees. We wanted these things to go well, we might have tried hard (or not) to get them to turn out well, and we wish they had in fact turned out as we had hoped. Human action is goal directed, and truth is no exception. We want to get things right. We target truth though we do not always hit the target. Failure frustrates but success gives us a sense of freedom, of power. What sort of power? It is not the power to dominate but instead the power to let oneself be bound by its claim.

There Is Truth

John Searle criticizes phenomenology for not beginning with what he calls the "basic facts" of physics, biology, and neuroscience. Phenomenology, it is true, begins by neither endorsing nor rejecting contemporary theories, whether philosophical or scientific; it holds them at bay as items of potential investigation and confirmation. It regards them as suggestions rather than facts. In doing so, it does not presume to do science but instead to make sure those who speak on behalf of science do not surreptitiously undermine the possibility of truth. For phenomenology does begin with a basic fact, and that is this one: *there is truth*, or, if you prefer, *truth happens*. This might seem to be so obvious, trivial in fact, that it hardly merits particular focus. But the claim of phenomenology is that truth is the sort of thing that must be sorted out first, on its own terms, to be what it is. If you try to make sense of it later, in terms of certain truths, say those of evolutionary biology or psychology, you end up generating problems of skepticism and relativism that undermine not just truth but all truths, including those of evolutionary biology and psychology. Science itself does nothing of the sort, but many scientists offer accounts of truth that make it into something merely subjective and relative. We hear accounts that reduce experience into sociological, psychological, biological, or physiological categories. If truth is nothing but a biological event, then every truth is a truth relative to biology. As Nietzsche puts it, "Between ourselves: since no one would maintain that there is any necessity for men to exist, *reason*, as well as Euclidean space, *is a mere idiosyncrasy of a certain species of animal*, and one among many."[1] Phenomenology thinks such a view is absurd. That a triangle's interior angles equal 180 degrees has nothing to do with our having the DNA we do. Of course, geometry would not have developed when it did if the Nile hadn't flooded annually, but that doesn't make the truths of geometry contingent on this historical fact. If we are to access truths independent of us, these essences cannot be bound up with humans as a natural species or with the idiosyncrasies of our history. Instead, truth must be bound up with that aspect of us that transcends these categories. It must be bound up with that part of us that can do sociology, psychology, biology, or physiology, not the part that is studied by these sciences. Phenomenology accepts the happening of truth and thereby rejects any such account that would undermine its validity.

Phenomenology arises in just this refusal to reduce truth to some contingent feature, in just this refusal to embrace the absurdity that truth is rooted in certain facts of human biology or psychology.

Husserl points out that there is no conflict between science and phenomenology but there is a conflict whenever scientists go beyond what science itself says and endeavor to philosophize (badly):

> In fact, we do *not* let *any* authority—not even the authority of "modern natural science"—curtail the legitimacy of recognizing every sort of intuition as an equally valuable, legitimate source of knowledge. If natural science actually speaks, then we listen eagerly and as apprentices. But natural science does

Phenomenology arises in just this refusal to embrace the absurdity that truth is rooted in certain facts of human biology or psychology.

not always speak when natural scientists speak, and certainly *not* when they speak about "philosophy of nature" and "epistemology befitting natural science."[2]

Why this hostility? In denying the experience of truth, these contemporary theorists destroy the reality of essences. Husserl continues:

> And, above all, *not* when they want to make us believe that the general kinds of self-evidence, such as all axioms express—propositions such as "a + 1 = 1 + a," "a judgment cannot be colored," "one of any two qualitatively diverse sounds is lower and the other higher," "a perception is *in itself* a perception of something," and the like—are expressions of experiential matters of facts, when we know all the while and in a *fully discerning manner* that propositions of this sort explicate and express givennesses of eidetic intuition.

What phenomenology will doggedly fight for is the reality of the experience of truth and of essence; any position that tries to explain this away is phenomenology's mortal enemy. Phenomenology clarifies how essences can arise in experience as transcending that experience. In this way, phenomenology is not opposed to the sciences; on the contrary, it is their greatest ally, for in clarifying the possibility of truth, it legitimates all the particular discoveries that happen in the sciences.

What is the condition for the possibility of truth? Truth happens in virtue of a fundamental openness marking the human being, an openness that offers a place for the things of the world to become manifest as the things that they are. The human is capable of a contemplative interest, an interest that allows it to relate to more than the environmental features relevant to survival and propagation. The human is capable of a contemplative interest that shatters the shackles of practical relevance, that sweeps upward to include the starry sky above, sweeps within to include the peculiar character of human existence, and sweeps wide to include an unlimited range of objects for investigation. The human is open in its being to the natures of things. This is the starting point of phenomenology, because it is the presupposition for all inquiry.

How does truth happen? First, it happens for someone. Truth is not anonymous but personal. If there is truth, it is because someone is responsible for bringing about its manifestation, for investigating, for seeing what there is to be seen. Truth is not something out there, something in databases or books; it is someone's insight. Yes, once truth has been registered, it can become uploaded and stored. One can, for example, learn many true things about "the Beatles" by reading Wikipedia. But of course each truth uploaded is the fruit of some anonymous fan's having registered that truth as such.

Second, truth happens for someone by making something present. That is, truth cannot be ascertained in the absence of the thing in question. It is in virtue of an investigation, of making something present, that we arrive at truth. Suppose someone says that San Diego is always sunny. It may be true or not. I go there in the month of June and experience what the locals call "June gloom." Every morning the sky is gray before it clears in the afternoon. Then I am in a position to know the truth. Or if I take something to be true that someone else has seen, I take it as true because it was present to that person. So if someone claims that the lost city of Atlantis exists, but she has not seen it, I won't regard her conviction as a case of truth. However, if someone says that Troy was a city that did exist, because she's seen the evidence, then perhaps I might regard it as true. Truth involves something's having been made present.

Third, truth happens for someone by making something present as it is. Naturally, presence, though important, is not sufficient. Something can easily be present but only in a confused way. Making present involves unpacking what is present in its constitutive features. It is a matter of mapping its part–whole structure. Someone is outside playing ball with his kids. He picks up the basketball to dribble it, but he finds that it hits the concrete with a hollow thud and returns not to his hand. The ball is not just present to him as a ball, but it is present as it is, that is, as a ball that is seriously underinflated.

So how can truth happen? Truth can happen because we are the sort of beings that are open in our very constitution, so that things can manifest themselves to us as they are. Heidegger and Husserl take us inside the spring of experience, down to its deepest tributaries in the temporal and spatial play of presence and absence.

Truth as Making-Present

Husserl says that in the experience of truth there is a characteristic fulfillment: *"The object is actually 'present' or 'given', and present as just what we have intended it*; no partial intention remains implicit and still lacking fulfilment."[3] Our flesh gives us a grip on the world; it affords a vantage point. Flesh enables things to be bodily present to us, enables us to move toward and about things and to see them as they are. Time—not the spatial representation of time on a clock, calendar, or graph, but lived time, the time of experience—gives us presence, a presence that bleeds forward into an immediately absent future and backward into an immediately absent past. The perception of anything unfolds temporally. I look at the Rodin sculpture in front of the Cleveland Art Museum. I've come out of the building and I see it from behind. Its front is absent to my gaze, but I walk around it. The back then present is now absent; the front then absent is now present. Time and my bodily being opens up this possibility. As the front comes into view, I gasp. This is not how Rodin's *The Thinker* is supposed to be. The legs terminate in twisted metal; the feet are missing! Instead of merely passively taking in my surroundings, a feature of those surroundings arrests my attention: What became of the thinker's feet? The fruit of this experience is the judgment, "Cleveland's copy of Rodin's *The Thinker* is missing its feet." I look for some explanation and see a sign reporting that in 1970 a bomb set by radicals exploded and damaged the sculpture.

Truth happened as I made Rodin's sculpture present as it is, as damaged. I could perform this feat of apprehension because I am open to the nature of things, an openness that involves the possibility of bodily exploration and the necessity of temporal distention. You can share in this truth by trusting me or corroborating my own act of making present with the making present of others. The speech of others consists of so many pointers of how things may be, of so many avenues toward things that we might take. Merleau-Ponty puts it this way: "Knowledge is not perception, speech is not one gesture among all the other gestures. For speech is the vehicle of our movement toward truth, as the body is the vehicle of our being in the world."[4] It is the meeting of speech and perception in the experience of

Figure 5 Cleveland's copy of Auguste Rodin's *The Thinker*. Photo © Chad Engelland.

truth that produces knowledge of things. Truth happens when our understanding of a topic is altered or confirmed by the topic's direct exhibition.

There's a tendency in the philosophical tradition and in everyday speech to think of truth as something that attaches to sentences or assertions that are made. So, in this way of thinking, an assertion is true if and only if it matches how things are. It is true that "Peter Piper picked a peck of pickled peppers" only if in reality *Peter Piper picked a peck of pickled peppers*. Phenomenology does not wish to dispute the fact that some assertions are true and some are false and the true ones are true in virtue of reflecting the way things are. But what phenomenology wishes to do is to drill down into the very happening of truth, to say that the essential thing, which can easily be overlooked, is the event that makes the true assertion true.

And what is that event? The display of the way things are. The simple truth of *seeing* Peter pick the peppers is more original than the subsequent statement reporting what was seen. Truth happens thanks to our experience of things.

Seeming versus Being

We are naturally concerned with the difference between seeming and being. Consider our response to the politician or religious leader who turns out to be a fraud or the lover who seemed true but cheats. In philosophy, the ambition since Parmenides has been to strike through how things seem to how they are. Phenomenology can seem to be the study of appearance or seeming rather than the study of how things are, being. In this way, it almost appears to be anti-philosophical. As we noted above, however, phenomenology in fact concerns true appearance, matched as it is to being. But why pay any attention to seeming and appearing at all? Why not just get to the things themselves?

While beach camping, my wife called to our children and said, "Look! It's a dolphin!" Out at sea, we saw the dorsal fin break through the water. There was general excitement. My daughter announced that dolphins were her favorite animals. Several minutes later, the dolphin appeared not to have moved; merrily was it surfacing and diving in one and the same place. Perhaps, we thought, that's not a dolphin. What was it? I looked through the binoculars and concluded that it appeared to be some trash. About an hour later the item washed ashore. Then we could see that it was in fact not a dolphin or a piece of trash, but a dead sea lion. The "dorsal fin" was in fact a flipper. In this case, how it seemed appears to be opposed to how it is, except for one thing. How did my family discover the truth? We finally got a good look at the thing. It was in virtue of this "good look" or "true appearance" that we could tell what it was. Husserl calls this an "adequate intuition" in contrast to an "inadequate" one. Adequate intuition clears up confusion and gives us the thing itself. "In an inadequate representation, we merely *think* that something is so (appears so), in adequate presentation we look at the matter itself, and are *for the first time made acquainted with its full selfhood*."[5] To take another example, we've all noted that a straw appears disjointed when it is in a glass filled with water. How do we know this is an inadequate presentation? By pulling the straw out and seeing that it appears straight. Only because we experience that the straw really isn't disjointed can we inquire into the properties of light and liquids that generate that appearance. It is always by true appearance that we can sort how something is from how it seems.

In false seeming, something appears as other than it is; in true seeming, something appears as it is. Of falsehood, Heidegger writes, "Similarly, 'Being false' . . . amounts to deceiving in the sense of *covering up*; putting something in front of something (in such a way as to let it be seen) and thereby passing it off *as* something which it is *not*."[6] At first it seemed to be what it is not—disjointed—before appearing as it is—intact. The question of the adequacy of the experience distinguishes the superficial and mistaken views of a thing with the deep and correct acquaintance necessary for truth.

Seeming and being are not necessarily opposed, for we can know of being in no other way than through true seeming. We cannot skip over how something appears to arrive at how it is; only through how it appears can we determine a thing's being. "Being essentially unfolds *as* appearing," observes Heidegger.[7] This alliance of seeming and being constitutes one of phenomenology's most significant contributions to philosophy.

Now, Searle thinks experience cannot be the final court of appeal for truth, but his criticism of the primacy of experience in fact makes tacit use of experience. He asks us to consider someone, we'll call him Jack, viewing an object; let's suppose it is a pair of sneakers. Unbeknownst to Jack, someone now interposes a mirror that reflects a different pair of identical sneakers, which appears in the same place. For Jack, they appear the same, so he takes them to be the same. Searle thinks that phenomenology cannot distinguish the two cases but that his method of logical analysis can. He writes from Jack's point of view: "I am no longer seeing the object I was originally seeing because that object is not causing my visual experience. The proof is that we *would not describe* this as a case of seeing the original object. This is straight, linguistic philosophy; it is not phenomenological analysis."[8] The problem with this critique of phenomenology is the ambiguity of his use of the word "we." *Who* would not describe it as the same object? Searle means us, the observers, who can see not only Jack and a pair of shoes, but the interposed mirror presenting to him a different pair. Searle is not coming up with a consideration that transcends experience. He is appealing to our experience, which has the appropriate vantage point for seeing the limits of Jack's point of view. Searle's attempt to claim an illusion on the part of phenomenology expresses a lack of sensitivity to his own implicit basis in experience. We cannot see beyond the limits of individual experience except by virtue of some other experience. Phenomenology has not been nor can it be outflanked.

Relativism

The word "truth" is a word that lately we have become suspicious of. We're not just suspicious of the truth espoused by those who stand to profit from it as in ages past. We are suspicious of its very idea. For starters, it seems unobtainable; all we can do is make guesses; everything we are given seems to be nothing more than mere appearances. Also, it seems somehow impolite to insist on the truth; opinion is more appropriate for our diverse world. Finally, we wonder in our heart of hearts whether truth is at all desirable; truth seems to hem us in, to limit our freedom—let us hear no more about truth!

But there's something less than exhilarating about a life lived under the banner of such resignation. It's like playing or watching a game in which no one tries to score; perhaps it seems impossible, maybe impolite, maybe confining; who says, after all, that soccer should be about scoring goals? If the players instead adopt some other approach, say, deciding that their only goal is to have no goals, the spectator and the players will soon lose interest. Sure, things might happen: a player goes here and then there, but there is nothing decisive, nothing to cheer about. What does a life look like in which truth is no longer a goal?

It's a life in which only appearances obtain. Is this not the life that phenomenology, the study of appearances, makes us live? To say that truth involves a *relation* between things and us does not mean that truth is *relative*. Only sloppy thinking can equate relationality with relativity. Relativity equates appearance and reality; relationality distinguishes between genuine and false appearances. Heidegger points out that it is a silly mistake to think that in physics the theory of relativity is a kind of relativism when in fact it considers relation with the sole aim of preserving the in-itself of the laws of nature.[9] Consider a phenomenon like a lunar eclipse in which the Earth casts a shadow on the moon. The perception of such an eclipse, like the perception of a sunset, depends on the place of the observer. An eclipse that can be seen in the Northern Hemisphere won't be seen in the Southern. But this relationality of the eclipse to the observer does not compromise the reality of the eclipse. So it is with phenomenology; relating things to their appearance has the single-minded goal of *preserving* the reality of things. Though truth is *related* to human existence, this relation does not compromise the in-itself of truth: "But that does not mean to say that what is discovered in the truth would be subjective opinion; rather, precisely as discovered the being is so, just as it is!"[10] Only confused thinking would equate phenomenology's doctrine of intentionality with a kind of relativism.

Truth is a feature not of things or of us but of a modality of the relation of things to us in which things show themselves as they are and are registered by us as such.

Truth then is not a feature of things independent of being thought, but thought does not make things be true; things make thoughts be true. As Aristotle said, "It is not because we think truly that you are pale, that you *are* pale, but because you are pale we who say this have the truth."[11] Phenomenology recovers this classical understanding that truth is a feature not of things or of thoughts but of the relation of thought to things, specifically, the subordination of thoughts to the self-showing of things. Our thoughts match things when things are allowed to take the lead and manifest themselves as they are.

Husserl pins the blame for relativism on the failure to understand the experience of truth: "Such doubts are only possible as long as self-evidence and absurdity are interpreted as peculiar (positive or negative) *feelings* which, contingently attaching to the act of judgement, impart to the latter the specific features which we assess logically as truth and falsehood."[12] If, however, self-evidence is understood correctly as the experience *of things*, then relativism is quite obviously ridiculous. Truth does involve a feeling of satisfaction, but this feeling is attached to the achievement of insight into the public display of what's real. Relativism makes Hume's and Nietzsche's mistake of internalizing appearances, of making them private. But self-evidence is not private; it is the self-showing of something as what it is, a self-showing in principle available to all.

Phenomenology finds the virtuous mean between two extremes. On one extreme is that of relativism: truth is simply appearance. Whatever happens to appear true is true. On the other extreme is that of misguided rationalism: truth has nothing to do with appearance. The virtuous mean holds that truth is a specific kind of appearance, one in which how the thing appears expresses how it is. Yes, things can appear as other than they are, but they can also appear as they are, and the latter is where truth occurs. Phenomenology as a doctrine of experience shows us how to sort seeming and being and thereby it deals a devastating blow to the doctrine of relativism, which regards seeming as the best available. What is so powerful about the phenomenological refutation is that it meets relativism on what is supposed to be its own turf—experience. Truth really does arise for us in and through experience.

We say we find an argument compelling, and the choice of that word is curious. Ordinarily, we don't think of freedom as relevant to truth, and yet it is the case, as this use of compelling suggests, that in the face of truth we are bound, compelled, determined, and that, in effect, truth binds us, shapes us, forces us. Are we not free in the face of truth? Or are we in effect enslaved by it? Truth compels us by freeing us. We experience the discovery of truth as liberation from ignorance; if we resist the truth we resist it not because it is true but because it somehow

What is so powerful about the phenom- enological refutation is that it meets relativism on what is supposed to be its own turf— experience.

makes life more difficult for us. But simply as truth, we find it binding, and yet being bound by it is not confining but instead opens us up. We feel compelled negatively by the bully or tyrant who wants us to say that what is x is not-x and thereby to violate the truth we see. We're supposed to say he has clothes even though it is evident he has not. But we feel compelled positively and indeed joyfully by the truth we see. It is good because true to say, "The emperor has no clothes!" We are free to submit to the truth, and that submission confirms our freedom.

At the heart of phenomenology is a twofold account of truth: truth cannot be identified with any psychological, neural, chemical, or physical process under pain of self-defeating relativism; truth nonetheless does require experience, the self-givenness of the state of affairs to the human being. What is the human being? Phenomenology calls for a new understanding of what it means to be human, namely, that being who experiences the truth of things. Referring to phenomenology as the "science of absolute honesty," Heidegger writes,

> The science of absolute honesty has no pretensions.
> It contains no chatter but only *evident steps*;
> theories do not struggle with one another here,
> but only genuine with ungenuine insights. The
> genuine insights, however, can only be arrived at
> through honest and uncompromising sinking into

the genuineness of life as such, in the final event only through the genuineness of *personal life* as such.[13]

We are summoned to phenomenology in our very being, and we are summoned to be truthful not only about things but also about our lives and our philosophizing.

LIFE

To taste a slice of freshly baked bread crowned with a pat of butter is not only to taste the bread and the butter but to taste oneself as alive and the recipient of that experience. To look out upon a lake and the sheen of the water mirroring the trees on the other side is to look also upon oneself as the live viewer of the scene. Right there in the tasting, in the viewing, there is an implicit, background experience of oneself. And were it not for this self-experience we would not relish the experience of these other things; we would not avidly seek them out to enjoy them. Our motive to experience would evaporate. It might just as well be someone else experiencing if the self were not in play. The phenomenologist Michel Henry emphasizes that life is grounded in this experience of oneself.[1] Every experience involves a nascent sense of oneself as agent of the experience.

Now, it is precisely in virtue of being alive, of having this experience of life from the inside, that one can perceive the life of another. Life can be perceived by life only in the mirroring of self and other made possible by the twofoldness of flesh: we perceive ourselves perceiving and we perceive others perceiving. In this way, Edith Stein argues that a nonliving observer, say, an alien robot, would be able to track mechanical movements but would be blind to the life expressed in that movement.[2] Here we can see the philosophical limitation of biology as the universal approach to life. Only insofar as biology as a methodological postulate does not take account of life's affectivity will it regard life purely mechanistically, purely physiologically, purely outwardly. The philosopher learns from biology but situates its findings within a more comprehensive context defined by the experience of life, both outward *and inward*. The phenomenologist can make sense of the fact that when we encounter other people and other animals their life is on display, not merely their metabolic existence, which is not prominent, but their affective lives: I see the dog sad to see me go, happy to see I have returned, and keenly interested to discover who's at the door.

The Human Niche

What is it like to be a rock? The question is a nonstarter, for the rock has no share in experience. What is it like to be a watermelon? Again, we cannot put ourselves in the shoes of the watermelon just as we cannot put ourselves in the shoes of the rock. What is it like to be a bee? This at last is a live question, for bees do have some share of experience, and the share that bees have is obviously strange and interesting. Heidegger exerts some effort in trying to put himself into the shoes of a honey bee. He uses biological studies and experiential transposition to explore the question. His aim is not to understand the bee's life on its own terms but instead to better grasp our own lives by comparison. What is it about human experience that is distinct? Heidegger hazards the following three theses:

The stone (material object) is *worldless*;

The animal is *poor in world*;

Man is *world-forming*.[3]

At this point, we are likely to feel the worry expressed by a number of contemporaries: Is this contrast between the human and the animal not a kind of "species chauvinism"? After all, if dogs philosophized, they would philosophize that they differed in kind from other animals. But this counterfactual hypothetical in fact proves Heidegger's point. Dogs, dolphins, and chimpanzees don't philosophize, and they don't do science. They don't ask such questions. It is strange but true that human beings find themselves alone in the world of theoretical investigation.

What sort of difference is this one between humans and other animals? A difference in degree is accidental, just a matter of tweaking what is already there. Is this a difference in degree? If so, humans would not be that much different from dogs and dolphins. A difference in kind, however, is essential; we need new principles to explain it. Is this a difference in kind? If so, humans would be significantly different from dogs and dolphins, and we would have to appeal to new principles to make sense of the human. Between rocks and animals, there is a difference in kind. Is there another such difference between humans and other animals?

In maintaining that animals are poor in world, Heidegger is clear that the environments of animals are not as such poor; they are poor only when those various environments are compared with the human world of linguistic experience and truth. The point is the richness of the human world rather than the poverty of the animal. Bees navigate and forage by living out a range of relevance specified by the good of the hive. They notice sources of nectar but they don't contemplate the intelligibility of the flower or the beauty of the bloom; there are no bee botanists or bee poets. Now, this might seem like a trivial point. After all, there are no human drones or human hives. But phenomenologists are not calling attention to random

It is strange but true that human beings find themselves alone in the world of theoretical investigation.

differences between bees and humans. They are high-lighting the character of the fundamental difference that makes the observation of this difference possible. The bee or any other animal is inscribed within the domain of an environment. Humans, by contrast, can transcend their environment and dwell within world. As a result, they can compare one environment with another.

Here again we are suspicious of the claim. After all, can't we interact with dogs, dolphins, and chimps? Can't we play fetch with Fido? Are we not relating to the same ball? The answer is that of course we relate to the same ball, but we humans are the ones who can relate to the ball *as being a ball*, who can understand what makes a game *be a game*, and the like. We deal with the essences of things, what they are. The milieu of speech and the intelligibility it expresses involves a contemplative dimension out of Fido's reach. Heidegger writes,

> For it is *not* simply a question of a *qualitative otherness* of the animal world as compared with the human world, and especially not a question of quantitative distinctions in range, depth, and breadth—not a question of whether or how the animal takes what is given to it in a different way, but rather of whether the animal can apprehend something *as* something, something *as* a being,

at all. If it cannot, then the animal is separated from man by an abyss.[4]

So even though the human world and the environments of animals can overlap by including the same things, they include the same things under different aspects. The animal remains exclusively within a practical register; the human can from time to time enter into a contemplative one. Developmental and comparative psychologist Michael Tomasello writes,

> No apes in any kind of environment produce, either for other apes or for humans, acts of pointing that serve functions other than the imperative function. That is, they do not point declaratively to simply share interest and attention in something with another individual (Gomez 2004), and they do not point informatively to inform another of something she might want or need to know—as human infants do from very early in ontogeny.[5]

Infants point not only to what they want; they point to what they or their companions find interesting: airplane! Apes, by contrast, point only to what they want: banana! The human is world-forming in the specific sense that it can be receptive to the essences of things.

The human being is the only animal that we know of to tap into the domain of truth. What are we to make of this contemplative aspect of human existence? What is this peculiarly human openness to truth? One mistake that can be made at just this juncture is to think that openness to truth is a biological feature of a certain species, *Homo sapiens sapiens*. The botanist's or poet's perspective on the flower is not more illuminating than the bee's; the truth of the botanist or the poet is a truth bound up with human biology. Nietzsche thinks that what we call truth is really nothing but an expression of the environment our biology sets before us:

> It is no more than a moral prejudice that truth is worth more than mere appearance; it is even the worst proved assumption there is in the world. Let at least this much be admitted: there would be no life at all if not on the basis of perspective estimates and appearances; and if, with the virtuous enthusiasm and clumsiness of some philosophers, one wanted to abolish the "apparent world" altogether—well, supposing *you* could do that, at least nothing would be left of your "truth" either.[6]

Here Nietzsche is on the verge of the phenomenological insight that truth is adequate appearance, but instead he sees appearances to be nothing more than a function of human biology. Phenomenology, by contrast, relates appearance and truth by virtue of distinguishing openness to truth from human biology. Things can indeed appear as they are; when they do we have the truth. The postmodern theorist Jacques Derrida sides with Nietzsche against phenomenology:

> It is evident that the difference between Nietzsche and Heidegger is that Nietzsche would have said no: everything is in a perspective; the relation to a being, even the "truest," the most "objective," that which respects most the essence of what is such as it is, is caught in a movement that we'll call here that of the living, of life, and from this point of view, whatever the difference between animals, it remains an "animal" relation.[7]

According to Nietzsche and Derrida, then, there is nothing distinctive about the human and thus nothing transcendent about truth. Who's right about truth? This is one of those cases where phenomenologists find it helpful to appeal to argumentation in order to defend the reality of experience. The Nietzsche–Derrida thesis has the absurd result of destroying truth and thus its own basis as a claim to truth. The evolutionary history of *Homo sapiens sapiens* is only accidentally true; it has to do with the peculiar features of the African savanna and the selection of chance mutations on the basis of adaptive advantage. However, the truth of essences is not accidentally true; the fact that $2 + 2 = 4$ or that H_2O is water or that leading is not the same thing as managing has nothing to do with human biology and the accidental details of our natural history. We could have evolved as winged amphibians on the shores of the Amazon and such truths would be equally true. Hence, against Nietzsche and Derrida, it must be maintained that we humans are tapping into something that transcends the idiosyncrasies of our biology and our environment when we tap into truth.

What is going on in truth? Phenomenologists point out that each of us is responsive to the truth that arises in experience. Heidegger follows Augustine in suggesting that we are at bottom constituted by *care* for the truth.[8] Things matter for us: our own lives, the lives of others, and the things themselves. We find ourselves beholden to their truth. To be human is to be a being bound by truth, to be a being in possession of the freedom to explore things as they are. Heidegger spends a lot of time unpacking the dynamics of this care as well as its roots in the very temporal structure of experience; the interplay of presence and absence allows truth to occur for us.[9] Of course, we can shrink from the truth of things and ourselves, obstinately dwelling superficially among the topics of our lives. Or we can face the truths of things and ourselves, resolutely dwelling thoughtfully with things. Phenomenologists take to calling the shallow mode "inauthentic" and the deep mode "authentic." It is only by being thoughtful that we come into our own and have ourselves, and "authentic" has the same root word, auto-, or self, as does autobiography. By contrast, when we are inauthentic, our story is written by others, by the mass media or trends on social networking. To live a human life is to choose continually between being faithful to the truth we have seen and not being so faithful.

How does our openness to truth interface with our animality and biology? Phenomenology repeats Socrates's classic distinction between condition and cause, and it follows Aristotle in thinking that the cause transforms the meaning of the condition.

1. Cause: that which determines the meaning of a thing

2. Condition: that which enables but does not determine the cause[10]

One could have very similar biological conditions, say, that of a bonobo and that of a human being, but insofar as these conditions are pressed to serve different ends, the biology of each has a different meaning. Our defining feature as humans is world openness or truth, and this means that even our hands are not merely for grasping but also for pointing things out.

We could not do biology and listen to music if we didn't have a lot of biology functioning in the background. We could not philosophize and debate if we weren't metabolizing and respiring, if neurons weren't firing, and if our ancestors long ago hadn't found a way to make a living on the African savanna. But none of these conditions constitutes the *cause* of our biologizing and philosophizing; none of these things explains our peculiar aptitude, our peculiar interest, our peculiar openness to truths that transcend our environment because they characterize the world. If it hadn't been for evolution, we wouldn't be here. But it is thanks not to evolution but to the domain of truth that we can register that fact—or any other. Human biology is a necessary but not sufficient condition for explaining our ability to do biology as a science.

Dwelling in the Lifeworld

To be human is to dwell within the lifeworld, which is the world of everyday things and ordinary perception.[11] Consider our experience of a kitchen table, which stands ready to serve as the locus for many meals, gathering about it humans to sup and supporting the food upon which they feast. The table, fashioned from sturdy materials, belongs to a web of significance: its design reflects the upright posture of our bodily frames, the convenience of having food nearer to hand and mouth, and the distance, partly for health and partly for self-understanding, between our feet that traverse the earth and the hands that bring food to our mouths. But it also reflects the fact that as a biological necessity we need to eat and as a personal necessity we wish to do so with others. The table speaks of our poverty, our needs, but also our aspirations, our hopes. It therefore testifies to that curious conjunction Hans Jonas identifies as a mark of life in general and human life in particular, namely, our "needful freedom."[12] The table—a standing flat surface for keeping things at a handy distance—is what it is in light of what we are.

Now consider the difference between the above experience of the table and the scientific account of the same table. What's real about the table is only that which we can measure, its dimensions and its mass. Ernest Rutherford observed that only a small percentage of alpha particles were rebuffed by gold foil, and he surmised that atoms are mostly empty save for their dense cores and orbiting electrons. His "planetary" model of the atom replaced Sir J. J. Thompson's "plum pudding" model. The sturdy table that keeps our fork at a handy distance when we reach for our water glass is in fact mostly empty space. According to the scientific model, the table is a mostly hollow mathematical body.

On the one hand, then, the table appears to be a solid piece of furniture that has a meaningful place within the ambit of human life; on the other hand, the table appears to be a mostly empty object having certain mathematical properties. If we compare the table around which we dine with the table modeled by science, we might wonder any number of things. Is the solidity of the table an illusion? Is the meaningfulness of the table a subjective projection onto something that is intrinsically bereft of meaning?

Let's look at the assertion, "Tables are not really solid." In making the assertion we are referring to *tables* and we know what we are referring to because we have perceived them. So, for the sentence to be *about* anything, we have to presuppose the reliability of perception in giving us a grip on the things that are. But note further that when we model tables scientifically we are no longer modeling tables in particular but instead a more generic object in general. What science tells us about tables is what science tells us about any similar material thing—a chair, a bed-frame, a dresser, firewood, or what have you. The scientific object does not tell us about the tableness of the table but only that out of which the table is made, its material substrate. Hence if we are to say, "This table is not really solid," we are missing the target. The table is solid, but its solidity corresponds on the atomic level to a substrate that, like a ping pong ball or Easter egg, contains mostly empty space. We should not puzzle about this, for a thing does not have to have the same properties as its substrate. No American is a member of the United Nations, but the

United States itself is, and no cell in a person's body is capable of taking a stroll, but a whole person is. A table can have different properties than the stuff out of which it is made.

The physicist Stephen Hawking said this about his three children and three grandchildren: "They have taught me that science is not enough. I need the warmth of family life."[13] The life of a family, the life lived, among other things, around the kitchen table, appears as a welcome "warmth" in contrast to the coldness of science. The scientific object, known via measurement and modeling, is divorced from our human lives; the lifeworld of everyday things, by contrast, is a place in which we can really dwell, for in the lifeworld is the flesh thanks to which we are present to our loved ones rather than merely spatiotemporally juxtaposed; in the lifeworld is the speech thanks to which we can talk about the things that really matter—the dinner to be shared or the life to be renewed; in the lifeworld is the experience of truth that challenges us and that vivifies us; in the lifeworld is the love that enables us to see what's truly good; in the lifeworld, too, is the wonder that gives rise to science, poetry, and philosophy. The contrast between the lifeworld and science is not the difference between feeling and fact, but the difference between experience and experiment, between the directly perceived world of life and the indirectly modeled world of measurement and mass.

The contrast between the lifeworld and science is not the difference between feeling and fact, but the difference between experience and experiment.

We do not piece together the lifeworld out of scientific objects; scientific objects, rather, are built out of the lifeworld; they are mathematically idealized and modeled representations achieved by human inquirers against the inconspicuous backdrop of dwelling in the lifeworld. Scientists make their discoveries surrounded by instruments and other people. Their work in the lab seamlessly integrates with the lunchtime conversations they have with colleagues. In the lab, they might go to a table and consult an electron microscope. They perceive the instrument and its controls, and they view its screen to see the images it produces. Even as they make startling discoveries about what things are made of thanks to their measurements, they must relate to their instruments and each other through the lifeworld of perception. In this way, the phenomenological and the scientific complement each other, being approaches rooted in either directly experienced structures or indirectly modeled material substrates.

Responsible for the Life of Another

In *The Mascot*, Alex Kurzem relates the inconceivable but real-life story of a Jewish boy who becomes a poster-child for the Nazis. The fateful turn of events comes when some German soldiers happen upon the boy hiding in an old schoolhouse. The boy looks at the leader of the soldiers and cries out, "I am hungry."[14] That cry of affectivity touches the soldier. He takes the boy inside and when he emerges moments later, he preserves the truth of the boy's dignity by lying to his fellow Nazi soldiers; he tells them that the boy is not circumcised. As a result, the boy's life is spared, and the regiment adopts him as its mascot. He appears in Nazi propaganda films as a model German youth.

The Jewish phenomenologist Emmanuel Levinas suffered through the same war in a Russian prisoner of war camp. That experience and that war saddled him with the terrible question concerning the inhuman way in which humans treat one another and its contrast with the way they are obliged to treat one another. As a phenomenologist, he wants to identify the dynamics at work in our experience of our obligations to others. He wants to take us inside the experience of the German soldier who discovers his responsibility for the Jewish boy, and who is moved to risk his own life to protect the life of that child. Levinas names this experience of the other's absolute claim "the face." In the experience of someone's affectivity, there is the experience of a face turned toward me. It is just this awareness of the other's vulnerability that elicits my unconditional responsibility. "The face is what one cannot kill, or at least it is that whose *meaning* consists in saying: 'thou shalt not kill.'"[15] Gabriel Marcel notes a similar experience when viewing the sleeping child whose radical vulnerability engenders a total responsibility felt by every feeling parent: "We might say that it is just because this being is completely unprotected, that it is utterly at our mercy, that it is also invulnerable or sacred. And there can be no doubt at all that the strongest and most irrefutable mark of sheer barbarism that we could imagine would consist in the refusal to acknowledge this mysterious invulnerability."[16] In the face of the other, each of us experiences our own unshakable responsibility. Rather than a burden, such an experience sets us free to act in a way charged with purpose and meaning.

Levinas observes, "Thus in expression the being that imposes itself does not limit but promotes my freedom, by arousing my goodness."[17] The experience of the other's vulnerability and my corresponding responsibility gives meaning to the power I feel within me and motivates me to bring it to completion. The soldier that rescues the boy feels the thrill of being bound to the truth of the child's absolute value and of acting accordingly. The life that we feel, the life there in every experience, the life on display in those we encounter, is a life responsive to truth, a life responsive to what things are and the claims they make on us.

LOVE

Among all the irrational forces that overwhelm the human, none seems as powerful and capricious as love. Tsunamis, earthquakes, and gale force winds are "out there," but love stirs inside us to shake us, twist us, and leave us quite turned about. Our pop stars and cultural prophets complain about this force and how it promises everything while delivering nothing; love seems suffused with illusion, to be little more than the fluff of sentimentality or the veil of lust. What is love? No less a poet than Shakespeare, in the play *A Midsummer Night's Dream*, presents it as a kind of magic-induced madness so powerfully deceptive that it will lead a beautiful woman to fall for a man with the head of an ass. Love seems to be a matter of losing your wits, of falling prey to illusion. It seems to be all sheen and no substance.

It is at this juncture, however, that phenomenology says something strange. Heidegger writes, "We are in the habit of saying that 'love is blind.' Here, love is regarded as an urge and so is replaced by an entirely different phenomenon. For love really gives sight."[1] It is the biological urge or the selfish sentiment that blinds us; love, by contrast, constitutes a fundamental openness to the beloved. Love lets us see what is there to be seen; it lets us succumb to the very being of the beloved. Phenomenology is the thoroughgoing enactment of the radical insight that love lets us receive things as they are.

Indeed, John Paul II quite perceptively characterizes phenomenology as "an attitude of intellectual charity."[2] It opens us up to the truth of things and the truth of others. What we don't care about we won't take the trouble to experience deeply. We'll instead rest content with superficial opinions and prejudices. Phenomenology lets us discover the truth of love. In doing so it frees us to uncover the truth of things.

We can miss what's happening in love when we think about it as a relation between two things: the lover and the beloved. Love is in fact a way of taking in the *whole world*, that is, the whole world as seen through the eyes of the beloved. Heidegger notes that the joy we experience in the presence of others is a joy we feel in the way the world is manifest to them: "Another possibility of such manifestation is concealed in our joy in the presence of the human existence—and not simply the person—of a human being whom we love."[3] We love the affectivity of our loved ones, not only their looks but also the way the world looks to them. Their look enhances our appreciation and understanding of things. The world bathed in the light of their love is a world washed of stultifying obviousness and freshly revealed in its charm.

Consider, in this regard, the renewal of life that comes from having children. Merleau-Ponty observes, "In the household where a new child is born, all objects change their sense, they begin to anticipate from this child some still indeterminate treatment; someone new and someone additional is there, a new history, whether it be brief or long, has just been established, and a new register is open."[4] The child's wonder before the world is contagious. It is not just the child that is a delight but also the new interest in the world, as a new understanding slowly dawns. We rediscover the living waters that swirl about below the ice whenever we speak and think about things, for children must figure out how to break into speech and come to understand things, and in minding their efforts we are brought to realize how strange it is that speaking happens or that inklings of illumination about things can occur and be shared.

Nietzsche suggests that love collapses in on itself, finding satisfaction not in the beloved but instead in its rapturous feeling: "In the end one loves one's desire and not what is desired."[5] Phenomenology replies that love draws one out of oneself, prompting one to find joy in sharing the beloved's world with the beloved. As one continues to learn to see the world through the beloved's eyes, one acquires new modes of insight. One doesn't just take note of something, such as sushi; one develops a way of thinking about it, evaluating it, enjoying it. One doesn't just take note of Avenger movies; one gets a sense of their specific excellence and the ingredients for a stellar and not-so-stellar installment of the franchise. In this way, love opens one up to the goodness and truth of things.

Amo, Ergo Cogito

The most famous line in all of philosophy is Descartes's signature phrase, *Cogito, ergo sum*, *I think, therefore I am*. While phenomenology cherishes the radicalness with which Descartes approaches philosophy, it constitutes a thoroughgoing critique of his starting point, beginning with the question of the *cogito*, or I think. Scheler expresses the critique powerfully: "Man, before he is an *ens cogitans* or an *ens volens*, is an *ens amans*."[6] To be a being that loves is to be a being open to the things of the world, things that can subsequently be known or chosen. Love is what makes the intentional relation possible; it is the spring at the heart of experience that phenomenology seeks to identify and release:

In our account love was thus always the primal act by which a being, without ceasing to be this one delimited being, abandons itself, in order to share and participate in another being as an *ens intentionale*. This participation is such that the two in no way become real parts of one another. What we call "knowing," which is an ontological relation, always presupposes this primal act of abandoning the self and its conditions, its own "contents of consciousness," of *transcending* them, in order to come into experiential contact with the world as far as possible. . . . Thus, *love* is always what awakens both knowledge and volition; indeed, it is the mother of spirit and reason itself.[7]

Love orients us in the world and allows for some things to be interesting and some things not.[8] The whole shows up to love in a variegated way, colored by that love. The specific complexion of the whole is called the *ordo amoris*, or order of love. We can describe what someone loves, what one takes an interest in, but we can also contrast that description with what one *does well* to love and take an interest in. Various kinds of illusions threaten. First, there is the possibility of loving something of relative value as if it were of absolute value. Here we have the hoarder who cherishes bottle caps as if they were the best things there are. This is *idolatrous love*. Second, there is the possibility of loving something of lesser worth over something of higher worth. Here we can think of the executive who prizes monetary gain over patriotism, shuttering a profitable local factory to make even more money overseas. This is *inverted love*. Third, there is the possibility of loving something with an intensity that falls short of its worth. Here we can think of the merely abstract appreciation that many have toward high culture, toward science, poetry, philosophy, and the liberal arts. This is *inadequate love*.[9] The *ordo amoris*, then, is not only descriptive but also prescriptive. One of the marks of thoughtfulness is to ask not only "What do I love?" but "What (really) is lovable?" and to take cues from exemplary people to challenge the horizon of love within which I see, think, and choose. The witness of the hero or the saint reveals to us new horizons of love. There is Henry David Thoreau challenging enthralled Americans to simplify their desires and draw inspiration from the quiet beauty of natural rhythms. There is Mother Teresa, her diminutive figure barely visible behind the UN podium in New York, audaciously bearing witness before the nations of the world to a love of those who are marginalized and powerless. Confronting a Thoreau or a Mother Teresa is so terrifying because their love threatens to transform our own secure but inadequate, inverted, or idolatrous loves.

When we think about the order of love, it is natural for us to think of love as love of others. Love is essentially altruism, so it is said, a concern for others over and above ourselves. Insofar as all human action requires a motive, we even doubt whether love is possible, for, as we tell ourselves, lovers always receive some satisfaction in loving or they wouldn't love at all. The paradigmatic case of a fellow in a foxhole throwing himself on a grenade to save his friends seems somehow tainted; after all, he must have felt that that was the noble action and thereby have had the subjective satisfaction of dying nobly. But phenomenologists reject altruism out of hand as the expression of vice, not virtue. It is arbitrary to prefer another to yourself for no other reason than that the other is not you; it is the flipside of egoism, which arbitrarily prefers yourself. Scheler writes, "If I myself am not worthy of love, why should the *'other'* be? As if he were not also an 'I'—for himself, and I 'another'—for him!"[10] To prefer the other for being other is to express an aversion to oneself. But love of another is not based on aversion. Therefore, altruism is not love. It instead expresses a kind of pathology, which leads us to busy ourselves with the affairs of others in order to avoid our own unwelcome selves. Scheler calls altruism "a nihilistic demand which destroys all vitality and indeed decomposes any structure of being!"[11] The order of love does not require preference for the other as other. Love doesn't require denying one's own interest in helping the beloved. Love sets aside ulterior motives, but it is essential to love to delight in loving. The subjective satisfaction doesn't undermine love, although it does reveal "altruism" to be a sham ideal. The friend lays down his life for his friend out of love, because he wishes to save his friend and because he wishes to be that sort of friend, the friend that loves to the end. To love another requires rightly loving oneself, of having a right self-regard.

How can we distinguish higher and lower objects of love? The distinction arises in the field of experience. Lower goods are goods that leave us empty when sought as though they were higher goods; higher goods are goods that leave us full when sought as though they were higher goods. When we prize physical pleasure above all, for example, we are left more and more desperate.

> The sensualist is struck by the way the pleasure he gets from the objects of his enjoyment gives him less and less satisfaction while his driving impulse stays the same or itself increases as he flies more and more rapidly from one object to the next. For this water makes one thirstier, the more one drinks.[12]

Consider the sort of emptiness that comes from binge-watching shows or internet indulgences. Lower goods leave one restless; higher goods open new depths of satisfaction. Consider the sort of fulfillment that comes from getting a job done right, such as installing wiring for a ceiling fan, or that comes in making a savory dish for a friend.

Alienation and Shame

Jean-Luc Marion argues that at bottom the only question that truly concerns us is the question, "Does anybody love me?"[13] And it is such a question for us because we are so routinely buffeted by (unloving) assaults on our person—by betrayals, indifference, and hostility. Consider if you will the typical grade school experience of mortifying shame when the teacher intercepts and reads to the class a note in which some disclosure is made, either an unkind remark or the avowal of some crush. The sharing of one's own thoughts or pictures to a public greedy to consume them as objects of curiosity, gossip, and ridicule is an all too frequent experience in an electronic age. What is at work in today's vigilance over privacy and outrage over accidental public disclosures? We want to be known, do we not? Why worry about *personal* things being known beyond our own intimates? What is so hateful about the experience that we can become destroyed by shame?

Jean-Paul Sartre says shame amounts to the experience of being objectified by others in such a way that their points of view threaten my own. I am a subject that views you as an object; conversely, you are a subject that views me as an object.[14] The attempt at reciprocal objectification engenders a fruitless dialectical tension, a kind of mutual assured destruction of subjectivity and with it a loss of freedom and dignity: "My original fall is the existence of the Other."[15] In shame, those indifferent to our being relate to us not as fellow subjects but as specimens or cases for comment and criticism. Sartre gives the famous example of looking in a keyhole to spy on someone and then, at the sound of footsteps, of shrinking in shame at having been caught doing something so unseemly; the objectifying voyeur becomes objectified! If love allows us to see the beloved as a point of view on the whole, shame shackles the shamed to being nothing more than an (unsightly) part of the whole.

Other phenomenologists, such as Scheler, note that shame can have a silver lining. In doing so, they are speaking not about guilt or shame felt in the eyes of others as a result of doing something shameful—Sartre's voyeur—but about the experience of being wrongly objectified—the voyeur's object of intrigue. The experience is negative, but its very negativity testifies to a truth of the human person, namely, that we are the sort of thing that should not be objectified; there's more to us than meets the objectifying eye. "Shame is a *protective feeling of the individual* and his or her value against the whole sphere of what is public and general."[16] Only because the person is a great good does shame arise. Shame is the "'anxiety' of the individual over falling prey to a general notoriety, and over the individual's higher value being pulled down by lower values."[17] Shame protects us from public objectification, and, in this way, it is allied with privacy. We are rightly known by intimates in love, not by those who do not have our interests at heart. That's why Chief Justice John Roberts correctly notes that a corporation like AT&T has no right to privacy. The corporation is a thing, not a person; it cannot be wrongly objectified or rightly loved. He joked, "We trust that AT&T will not take it personally."[18] Shame testifies negatively to what love registers positively, namely, that the person is not only a part of the world but also a point of view on the world.

The experience of shame also captures a tension written into our very character as flesh, that is, as one that receives the world of experience while simultaneously being a part of that world. This twofold character opens the possibility of our being reduced in the eyes of another to the mere anonymity of bodily parts.[19] Shame, however, reveals that our bodies are not analogous to slabs of meat. Instead, they are the outward face of our inward selves and are charged with personal significance.[20] The sexual feeling of shame arises due to the fact that love directs us toward the individual person but desire directs us toward bodily enjoyment. This difference between seeking the person and seeking bodily enjoyment makes it necessary to hide one's most intimate flesh before lust and reveal it only for love. The idea of spousal love is that the lover not only desires but loves the beloved, and consequently enjoyment does not undermine the twofold character of flesh; in the name of love, shame can therefore disappear.[21]

Another negative experience with a positive meaning is solitude. While standing in line, at a party, or even in one's own room, one can keenly feel alone. This need not have anything to do with feeling lonely, which is an experience of solitude marked by unrest; feeling alone can instead be perfectly peaceful. In that experience of solitude, one experiences one's own selfhood and its orientation to others. Such solitude is not something negative; it is a profoundly positive experience that lies at the basis of all communion with others. In solitude we experience ourselves as selves by ourselves; in communion we experience ourselves as selves together with others.[22] Communion cancels the absence characteristic of solitude by bringing about the presence of others. Only one who can be alone without being lonely can love another no longer incidentally—as an antidote to loneliness—but specifically as a welcome presence.

Loneliness turns to others as a distraction from self; authentic solitude enters into communion with others as a complement to oneself.

Participation and Dialogue

The look of a stranger not only threatens; it also beckons, welcomes, acknowledges. Sartre fails to see the positive possibility of love, and he thus sees the presence of others

Only one who can be alone without being lonely can love another no longer incidentally—as an antidote to loneliness—but specifically as a welcome presence.

as dangerous. The only possibility of encounter is alienation in which other people snatch my world from me by construing it relative to their own points of view. Other phenomenologists, more attentive to the modalities of human experience, underscore the positive possibilities of human encounter. These modes of love include not only familial, spousal, and friendly love, but also solidarity; these are modes of participation, modes of sharing the world together. We experience the meaningfulness of being part of a whole.

Love begins in perceiving the value of the beloved. It comes to fruition in making a thoughtful gift of ourselves to promote the beloved's good. This happens through a sharing of not only thoughts, labors, and time, but also our flesh, including our animal inclinations. One of the most characteristic acts of friends is to share a meal together, satisfying simultaneously not only their need to eat and metabolize but also their desire for fellowship and conversation about life. It takes effort to hear, to follow the thoughts of another, but this is done gladly for one's friend, whose world has become an addition to one's own. Heidegger even speaks mysteriously but truly about how we carry the voice of our friends around with us, ever ready to listen to what they have to say whenever they are present to us.[23] To educate children is to tutor them in the works of love, the ability, among other things, to make good conversation over a meal or to pitch in constantly and without prompting in the works of love that contribute to the life of the family. Friends and family members share life, the life of our bodily needs and wants and the life of our highest aspirations for truth and goodness.

The Polish phenomenologist Karol Wojtyła develops a rich account of participation in the treatise *The Acting Person*, which he writes while suffering from the stultifying impersonal forces of communism.[24] To participate, he says, is to take part with other persons in joint activity as persons. Participation stands in the sharpest contrast with every view of the human as an anonymous cog in a wheel, every view that regards the human as a "resource" rather than a contributor, every view that reduces the person to a mere mechanical function, such as a paper pusher in a bureaucracy. Participants experience themselves as meaningful parts of the whole. They take delight in working for the good of the whole and thereby experience solidarity. Wojtyła notes that a participant might also sometimes need to voice opposition to the whole as the expression of an allegiance to the common good; precisely because I too belong to the whole, my thoughtful aversion to the dominant mindset needs to be shared. The whistleblower who exposes a culture of corruption will cause distress no doubt, but such opposition will prove to be the highest contribution to the good of the corporation and those whose needs it is supposed to serve. The interplay of solidarity and opposition promotes the sort of healthy dialogue necessary for social and political life. Such authentic attitudes stand in contrast to conformism and avoidance, which shun confrontation and with it the possibility that truth might become shared. When Wojtyła later became Pope John Paul II, he made a historic 1979 return trip to Poland in which he eschewed the inauthentic attitudes of conformism and avoidance and instead opposed the atheism of the communist regime: religion, he bore witness, belongs in the public discourse of Poland. He thereby energized the Polish Solidarity movement that undermined the communist hold on the country.

Such witness is not just important for views other than our own. Only a year earlier, Aleksandr Solzhenitsyn, who had been in exile in the United States for speaking out against communist oppression in his homeland of Russia, used the occasion of a 1978 speech at Harvard University to challenge the contemporary ethos of America. He boldly claimed that Americans had lost courage to confront dangers and had traded in the quest for higher goods for a comfortable but ultimately unsatisfying quest to consume as much as possible. Was he being simply cantankerous and ungrateful to his hosts? Or was he offering as repayment for America's hospitality the highest good he could, namely, testimony to the greater goods of the human spirit?

Phenomenology constitutes a timely reminder in an increasingly sectarian media environment of radically polarized rhetoric: that genuine dialogue, marked by openness to truth, is necessary for the good of all of us. In participation, I contribute myself to the good of the whole so that I don't allow the truth I see to be drowned out or hidden. Instead, I must propose it to others and welcome the claims of truth of others, especially when they contradict my own. Only by listening to the witness of others can we experience what they experience and turn, jointly, to the truth of the matter. Each of us might be wrong, but we cannot determine who that might be unless we mutually submit to the truth of the thing in question. Genuine participation is participation as persons, as perceivers of truth, in a shared conversation about the good of our various communities. Public discourse requires openness to truth in order to avoid devolving into the strident us-versus-them rhetoric of power and intimidation that aims at social conformism. Phenomenology invites us to see our political life together as susceptible to truth, which can be shared thanks to a dialogue concerning competing senses of what is truly lovable and good.

Love perceives the goodness of life and motivates the works that sustain, enrich, and celebrate it. In doing so, it joins our worlds one to another and forges a whole, protecting us from the alienating forces of objectification. It affords the context for truth, even challenging truths, to be shared, so that, conversing one with another, we might

Phenomenology invites us to see our political life together as susceptible to truth, which can be shared thanks to a dialogue concerning competing senses of what is truly lovable and good.

gradually grow in knowledge of the things that are. This sort of labor, the life lived together in the ambit of truth, requires courage and patience. It requires dedication and focus. It requires us to resist the anesthetizing allure of the superficial so that we might challenge each other to plumb the depths of experience in order to arrive at the truth of the matter.

WONDER

What do we do when we can do whatever we want to do? Young and old, rich and poor, introvert and extrovert do one thing and the same: either play or watch others play. We pick up a ball and bounce it, we get out a deck of cards, we play an instrument and sing; we watch a game, a play, or a movie. The fact that the beach offers so many avenues for play constitutes, no doubt, much of its draw. Now the notion of play may seem childish. But phenomenologists bring out its essential structure, a structure that involves the inner dynamisms of experience.[1]

Though play involves an absence of toil, it is not motionless but full of activity. When we work we endeavor to produce something we need or that proves useful. We make a meal or build a house. When we play we engage in an activity that has no use. It is an activity that we choose to do for its own advantage, because we enjoy it. (The extent to which we are able to enjoy our work is the extent to which we can achieve a sort of excellence and freedom from toil that approximates play.)

Phenomenologists focus on play because it involves a sense of external display; you can't make sense of it solely in terms of the "inner" attitudes of the individual players. After all, play is something that remains open to the experience of spectators, and spectators don't peer inside the players but instead see their outward display. The spontaneous play of a child elicits the interest of a parent, and the disciplined play of an athlete or musician elicits the interest of us all.

One of my earliest childhood memories is sitting on top of the monkey bars and calling to my mom, "Look at me!" I had conquered something, and I wanted my mom to see the deed. Our more formalized playful activities, sports, intensify this inclusion of others. Why do we want to watch others play? Why do players crave attention? We want to be able to bear witness to the truth we've seen. Nike captured this in a ten-story billboard in Cleveland emblazoned with the image of hometown hero Lebron James and the tag line, "We are all witnesses." (The billboard was hurriedly taken down in 2010 when he left for Miami, only to be erected again in 2014 when he returned and then removed again in 2018 when he left for LA.) In a game, the participants strive to achieve a kind of display that we might call glory. The game-winning, last-second shot from midcourt actually finds its target. It's incredible, and it's glorious. The spectacular play transcends the moment and presents the ideal. We marvel that what *is* in this case matches what *should be*, for so often it does not. We relive the moment, savor its sweetness, and honor its hero.

In a work of art, the participants strive not for glory but for another sort of display, beauty. Heidegger writes, "Appearance—as this being of truth in the work and as work—is beauty."[2] We don't watch the sculptor carving in the way we watch the player shooting. It is the result and not the activity that we witness in its glory. Sure, the young Michelangelo understandably chiseled his name in capital letters across the sash of the Madonna in his famous *Pieta*, just so everyone would know who carved it, but our focus is not on the carving but on the carved, the hunk of marble that magically transpierces our hearts with its truly exquisite beauty.

The glorious athlete and the beautiful artwork draw us out of ourselves. They put on display an exemplary excellence or an affective truth that resonates with our own nature. When we witness sports or art, we behold the wonder of being human. We are moved to contemplate the truth of what we are.

Bored with Ourselves?

We are usually quick to find something interesting or not. But what do we mean by this word? Heidegger distinguishes a deeper interest, which is charged with wonder, and a superficial interest, which is touched by boredom.

> [1] Inter-est means to be between and among things, to stand in the midst of a thing and to remain near it. [2] But today's interest accepts as valid only what is interesting. And interesting is the sort of thing that can freely be regarded as indifferent the next moment, and be displaced by something else, which then concerns us just as little as what went before. Today, one often takes the view that one especially honors something by finding it interesting. The truth is that such a judgment has already relegated the interesting thing to the ranks of what is indifferent and soon boring.[3]

The deeper interest actuates that human possibility of caring about something, of not being indifferent to it. The superficial interest remains indifferent to the thing in question; it is effectively placed on a conveyor belt that will soon carry it away to be replaced by something else of only momentary interest.

At first blush, it might seem we turn to distraction to avoid that thing called boredom. It makes sense that we'd want to run from *that*. But Heidegger alerts us that something deeper is going on. We are not so much running from boredom as we are from ourselves, from our own listlessness:

Why do we find no meaning for ourselves any more, i.e., no essential possibility of being? Is it because an *indifference* yawns at us out of all things, an indifference whose grounds we do not know? Yet who can speak in such a way when world trade, technology, and the economy seize hold of man and keep him moving? And nevertheless, *we* seek a *role for ourselves*. What is happening here?, we ask anew. Must we first make ourselves interesting to ourselves again? Why *must* we do this? Perhaps because we ourselves have become *bored* with ourselves?[4]

All our choices and our options have blinded us to the essential fact that we have lost the capacity to experience things deeply. We instead think of ourselves as consumers—as subjects who remain fundamentally indifferent to what is selected and consumed, who remain unaffected by the content. Originally it was not so. Experiences were transformative. We did not consume them; they consumed us. If modern life bores, it is for no other reason than experience has become turned inside out.

As we throw ourselves into this or that experience, we find again and again nothing but ourselves, our preferences, our judgments: I like this, I don't like that. But there remains another possibility, hard, very hard for us to fathom: to approach experience not as impassible bystanders but as active participants, to see ourselves as pilgrims rather than tourists.

Countering Disconnection

In a Samsung commercial, a young dog owner proudly shows his friend pictures of his dog doing a single back flip. Both are intently focused on the images appearing on his phone. The television camera pans out to show the viewer at home that right in front of them the very same dog is energetically doing a series of ever more amazing tricks, although the phone users remain oblivious to it. All too easily images stand in between us and things, even the very things they are images of. How can we be connected to everything and yet disconnected to what's there before our very eyes?

Technology gives us an awesome power, a power to have the world in our pocket and to carry with us the attention of hundreds of fellow travelers on life's way. But even as it satisfies so great a desire in us so that we cannot imagine life without it, that is not the whole story, for from time to time, we get a hint that something is missing. First, even though everything is always available to us, we remain strangely distant from the things around us and we register that fact dimly, as something on the verge of being remembered. We don't get the sense of intimacy and familiarity that we want. Second, technology is a veritable arms race to crowd out everything else; its designers want to hold our attention as long as possible. It's no wonder we feel that we just cannot let go of it. As Heidegger puts it, "We depend on technical devices; they even challenge us to ever greater advances. But suddenly and unaware we find ourselves so firmly shackled to these technical devices that we fall into bondage to them."[5] We feel unfree, and we know that's not right. Third, technology can't quite deliver what it promises. All our connections leave us strangely unsettled; we feel ourselves alienated, alone, unfocused, vexed, confused, and so very exhausted. From time to time, we feel that we live in what Marcel calls a "broken world," a world of artifice that lacks the joy of being: "The deadly boredom we find in the countries which are stricken by this cancer is bound up with a corresponding weakening of the sense of being, and with an increasing disappearance of joy."[6]

Phenomenology distinguishes between problems and mysteries. A problem is something that can be objectified (*pro-blema* has the same etymology in Greek as *ob-jectum* does in Latin: it means "to be thrown before" us). It can be isolated for focused investigation, and as such it can admit of a solution. A mystery, by contrast, is something that cannot be so objectified, because it cannot be isolated, and it therefore cannot be solved. The reason the mystery cannot be made into a problem is that the mystery includes, in its very subject matter, the investigator as investigator. When it comes to a topic such as flesh, language, or truth, we cannot put it under the microscope in the same way we might investigate any number of other things; we cannot do so, not because of some limitation in these topics or in ourselves, but because these topics are woven into our very selves and the very possibility of investigation. I investigate flesh, language, and truth only while making use of flesh, language, and truth. I must find, within the living of these dimensions, a way to clarify them and concentrate them. I must live them as a mystery in the technical sense employed by Marcel and Merleau-Ponty.[7] Mystery is not synonymous with enigma or unsolved problem. We can indeed make progress in clarifying these terms but only in such a way that they admit of further investigation and in such a way that we ourselves remain in question.

Experience is not amenable to problem-solving in the way that theoretical or practical hurtles can be surmounted by calculative thinking. There's no new app, gadget, program, or protocol for leading us into a more meditative engagement with the mystery of life. Nor is such meditation a retreat into the irrational or the mystical. Rather, it is a matter of becoming aware of the contours of experience and making a commitment to sharing the truth of the world through speech and flesh. There are certainly deeper dimensions to human experience, religious dimensions, that can thereby become available, but the phenomenological turn to a meditative thinking has nothing particularly mystical or religious about it. Rather, it is a matter of returning from distraction to dwell more thoughtfully with what will and won't fulfill us.

The Wonder of Things

Wonder admits of degrees.[8] Its first stirrings are subject to the gravity of boredom, but its higher enactment achieves escape velocity. At first, in everyday modes of wonder, something curious or strange appears against the backdrop of the usual. We are surprised by the plot twist at the end of the movie or by the new trend in fashion. Such a surprise is of course fleeting and, in hindsight, not surprising. A deeper mode is when something unusual emerges in its unusualness. Here lies our fascination with Hollywood celebrities, but such a fascination remains infected with gossip about them; they don't move us out of ourselves. Can you believe she's dating him? The deepest mode of everyday wondering happens before sports icons and heroes. Here we find ourselves confronted with something not only unusual but extraordinary, and we stand in awe, overwhelmed by the grandeur of the person in question. I cannot believe, we tell ourselves, that Chesley Burnett "Sully" Sullenberger III landed the engineless plane on the Hudson River, saving everyone on board. That's not just momentarily surprising, and it is not something that we can undermine with gossip. No matter how you slice it, it's an extraordinary accomplishment.

Heidegger points out that we often chase after the sensational because we're confused about what's really important. "Yet we are equally liable to pass by what is essential, if only because we so seldom possess the capacity for genuine admiration, and so seldom manage to open one another up to what really deserves our admiration, remaining strong in such admiration."[9] Beyond ordinary modes of wondering are more philosophical ones. There is the wonder of the scientist who endeavors to figure out why zebras have stripes. It turns out it has nothing to do with camouflage but may have to do with a strategy for frustrating the landing skills of horseflies.[10] It's the contrast between this actual striped feature and all the possible features it might have had in its place (polka dots, checkers, splotches, etc.) that provokes wonder. If we could only relate to the actual, there would be no wonder, no ability to ask why. Instead, we would just run up against fact after fact about how things are. But because we can understand what is in light of what might have been but isn't, the actual appears as what didn't have to be and thus as something that deserves an explanation for why it is the way it is.[11] How is scientific inquiry into causes possible? It is possible due to human transcendence, the fact that we don't just relate to facts but we see facts as they are against their not having to be as they are. That difference between actual and possible provokes our wonder: Why should it be this way and not another? Scientific inquiry is a fruit of human transcendence, the very reality that phenomenology endeavors to unpack and illumine.

The Wonder of Essential Knowledge

Admiral Grace Hopper, the notable mathematician and computer programmer, makes a strategic distinction in her 1986 retirement speech from the US Navy. She calls for more leadership in government research, saying, "You manage things; you lead people."[12] What is at work in her distinction between managing and leading? After all, we are in the habit of referring to mid-level employees as managers, not leaders. Note that in making this distinction she is reflecting on human affairs; she is not presently living the distinction. She is neither leading nor managing but reflecting. She has taken a step back, paused the living of life so to speak, in order to understand more deeply some of the terms in which human life together is lived. Her reflection does not drain life of significance; on the contrary, it enhances it.

How does she arrive at this distinction? Think about what it is to manage; it involves an exercise of care on the part of the one managing. We say that "we can manage

Scientific inquiry is a fruit of human transcendence, the very reality that phenomenology endeavors to unpack and illumine.

it" or "I've got it under control." In management, freedom resides in the one who puts things in order. But when it comes to other people, as opposed to things, there are now other freedoms at issue, other sources of order and creativity. To include these sources of freedom upsets the original sense of management; with other people there is now a sense of joint activity. Including other people, then, explodes the bounds of what it means "to manage" and becomes something else. What else? Well, the freedom of the person in charge must evoke the freedom of the others; it is one of inspiring or promoting. Hopper calls that leading. You cannot lead your affairs, for things, being unfree, are not capable of joint action; you cannot manage people, for people, being free, are capable of joint action. Hence you manage affairs and lead people. Hopper's point is that confusing managing with leading stifles the creativity necessary for fruitful innovation.

Philosophy is a rigorous intensification of ordinary reflection, and phenomenology is a renewal of philosophy. When we reflect, we take a step back from what we're doing in order to gain needed perspective on it. Stepping back opens a new kind of distance to the subject in question, and by opening up that distance, we make it possible to bring the thing close in a new way. We can then catch up with it in thought. For example, one of the most looked-up words on Merriam-Webster's website is "love."[13] This is not, of course, because people are looking for a linguistic definition; it's because when one is in the throes of love, it can often be deeply puzzling. We step back from a relationship and ask about the nature of relationships in order to come back to that relationship—or future ones—in a deeper or more thoughtful manner.

Since Socrates, philosophy has specialized in the natural human ability to take a step back from human affairs to clarify the terms at work in life so that we might more fully and intently live our lives together. For Socrates, it is a matter of formulating a definition that does not contradict itself or some truth of the matter. Phenomenology renews the Socratic method of defining by connecting it to experience; defining is a matter of clarifying or explicating the original experience of the topic of investigation. We must *envision* the essence of the thing to grasp what it is. Husserl calls it "eidetic intuition," because it is a way of grasping what something is (*eidos* in Greek). How does it work?

Think of the thing in question, put before yourself a preliminary understanding of its essential features, the features that seem to be necessary for it. Now go to work via imagination. Take each feature, one by one, and cancel it, put it offline, take it out of the picture. Does the thing remain the same thing when you do so? If it does, that feature wasn't essential; leave it out from your consideration. Does the thing change into something else when you do so? If it does, that feature was essential; put it back in and move on to the next. Eidetic intuition allows us to demarcate one thing from another. Note that it brings to experience the very same noncontradictory character that Socrates was the first to champion as the hallmark of essences.

Consider something like friendship. Gather together all the features of friendship and then begin to examine them. It seems like friendship requires reciprocity. Is that so? Well imagine a friendship without reciprocity. Jack befriends Jill but she does not reciprocate. That's not really a friendship, is it? Hence, reciprocity is an essential feature. What about this reciprocity? Could it amount to a situation in which there is reciprocal benefit? Is that enough to have a friendship? Jack is Jill's dentist, and Jill is Jack's accountant. They both benefit from the relationship, but is this reciprocity really enough to constitute a friendship? Here Jack is interested in Jill only for his own sake, and Jill is interested in Jack only for her own sake. This is a beneficial relationship, but it is not the sort of thing celebrated by the term "friendship." So friendship requires a deeper kind of reciprocity, one that's going to take an interest in other people themselves and not just what we can get out of them. Let's call this deeper reciprocity mutual goodwill; each wills the good of the other. Can we imagine a friendship that didn't have mutual goodwill? Could Jack and Jill be friends if they didn't will each other's good? Of course not. So mutual good will turns out to be an essential feature of friendship. If we are going to present to ourselves a friendship, it has to have mutual goodwill; that point is unvarying for all friendships.[14] Eidetic intuition identifies this feature of friendship as essential. Just as people can be logical without studying the science of logic, so people can be insightful without studying the phenomenological tool of envisioning essences. All the same, just as studying logic can improve one's native intelligence, so practicing the envisioning of essences can improve one's ability to grasp what things are while distinguishing them from what they are not.

The Wonder of Phenomenological Experience

Alongside the phenomenological enhancement of our thoughtful ability to think perceptively about things, there's also a specifically phenomenological form of wonder, glimpsed here and there by philosophers and fully lived out for the first time by phenomenology. Wonder can take other directions; for example, many a philosopher has wondered why anything should exist at all. But phenomenological wonder remains exclusively concerned with the marvelous nature of experience. The first variety of phenomenological wonder happens before the usualness of the usual, where the ordinary character of everyday experience appears in its strangeness. The things in the field of experience appear in the wonder of their appearing. How incredible, we say to ourselves, that experience should happen, that things should be present! A still deeper wonder, bound up with this first, is attentive to the absence involved in each and every presence. If I should wonder before the presence of things, I should also wonder about the absence that makes this possible; if the foreground of experience fascinates, I should allow myself to be transformed by the background that enables the foreground to come to the fore. Rather than everyday wondering about an unusual profiled against the usual, phenomenology invites us to wonder about the usualness of the usual itself. There is something enduringly startling, surprising, and strange about the field of experience and what it affords us.

The shift from boredom through genuine interest to wonder is the shift from things to their self-manifestation. Much like Heidegger, Husserl sees philosophy originate in the wonder that is the fruit of life at its most lively and playful:

Incipient theoretical interest, as wonder, is obviously a variant of curiosity, which has its original place in natural life as an intrusion into the course of "serious living," either as a result of originally developed life-interests or as a playful looking-about when one's quite immediate vital needs are satisfied or when working hours are over. Curiosity (here understood not as a habitual "vice") is also a variant, an interest which has separated itself off from life-interests, has let them fall.[15]

He says that a form of this wonder is the mother of phenomenology:

> The correlation between world (the world of which we always speak) and its subjective manners of givenness never evoked philosophical wonder (that is, prior to the first breakthrough of "transcendental phenomenology" in the *Logical Investigations*), in spite of the fact that it had made itself felt even in pre-Socratic philosophy and among the Sophists—though here only as a motive for skeptical argumentation. This correlation never aroused a philosophical interest of its own which could have made it the object of an appropriate scientific attitude.[16]

Phenomenology, then, is nothing other than the advent of a new wonder, the wonder before the truth of experience. Heidegger approaches this wonder through a bevy of related experiences: angst, joy, and even terror; what's happening here is a shift from things to the world of presence in which things appear.

Phenomenology is nothing other than the advent of a new wonder, the wonder before the truth of experience.

It did not escape the notice of classical philosophers that friends enhance our experience. Aristotle explains the goodness of good friends as follows: the presence of their goodness helps us perceive the goodness of being.[17] He writes, "Indeed, it is always the first sign of love, that besides enjoying some one's presence, we remember him when he is gone, and feel pain as well as pleasure, because he is there no longer."[18] Augustine, too, speaks of the way friends crave each other's presence and are averse to each other's absence.[19] It is not a desire for presence as such or an aversion to absence as such, but a desire for the presence of the friend. The beloved reveals to us the value of being and clues us in to the difference between presence and absence. Love takes us beyond indifference and boredom by bringing us into wonder, and it is this wonder that is the threshold for phenomenological analysis. Phenomenology recovers the classical insight of an Aristotle or an Augustine that resonates with the experience of each of us: it is good to be in the presence of friends. There is thus a way into phenomenology through love. Phenomenology must only distinguish the friend from the field of presence in order to begin.

Stages of Phenomenological Wonderment

Initiation into phenomenology involves coping with a strange vocabulary and novel claims. This way of speaking only gradually takes shape, shifting from something strange, to a way of speaking, to a way of thinking, and finally to a way of manifesting the truth of things.

Marveling Stage: First, there is provocation occasioned by hearing phenomenology's puzzling, counterintuitive negations, negations that unsettle but also promise something liberating, something that upsets the standard intellectual picture of ourselves and the world. What can it mean that experience does not take place in our brains? Can it really be true? It seems manifestly false. And yet, would that it were true. Phenomenology seems to promise just what I have been waiting for. Phenomenology reveals a tension between what I have always been told and what I had surmised to be true. In this way, phenomenological claims fall under a double judgment: they *can't* be true and they *must* be true. If I don't settle on the former but allow myself to be drawn in by the latter, I develop a hope that what phenomenology promises might yet prove true. I need to read more. I read phenomenological texts with fascination and yet thorough confusion.

Speaking Stage: In the second stage there is an enthusiastic miming of vocabulary, with many mistakes. This is the stage of most student papers. I am an amateur language-game speaker, and I take my bearings from the boldest claims of the phenomenological authors. In seizing upon this claim or that novel word and inserting it into my sense of the whole and operative vocabulary, I become accustomed to the phenomenological mode of thinking and speaking. In this way, phenomenological claims start to make some sense and take on a superficial plausibility. I know enough to want to know more and to think I know more than I do.

Thinking Stage: In the third stage I become an expert speaker of this new language game. I can echo its vocabulary flawlessly and can do so endlessly. I have as it were uploaded the logic of the phenomenological way of thinking. This is the stage of most dissertations. I read phenomenological texts with satisfaction: Here is how one *should* speak about the matter. Phenomenology has coherence, but it is the coherence of a model; it is a script for rigorous speaking, but I am not yet in a position to see that it rises to the level of truth.

Truthing Stage: In the final stage, I achieve fluency. Phenomenology is not just a way of speaking or of thinking. It is a way of accessing a whole class of truths. In this stage, I become an interlocutor who necessarily criticizes with understanding; criticism prior to this stage misses its target; there is a difference between fluency in a foreign tongue and fluency in one's mother tongue—the latter involves the ability to speak against and to speak better and certainly to speak other than the words one has heard. I read a phenomenological text as so many opportunities for confirmation and disconfirmation, as so many opportunities for elucidating the truth of things. And I can and do generate new phenomenological texts; I cannot help but to do so, for the words themselves arise in the presence of puzzling phenomena. I want—no, I need—to elucidate, to explicate, to phenomenologize.

Phenomenology is something we learn by doing; it is something that is first experienced and then afterward understood. Heidegger writes, "But what is most essential is first of all to have traversed the whole path once, so as, for one thing, to learn to wonder scientifically about the mystery of things and, for another, to banish all illusions, which settle down and nest with particular stubbornness precisely in philosophy."[20] *To learn to wonder scientifically about the mystery of things*—there is no better formulation possible about the peculiar quest of phenomenology, which seeks to clarify with all rigor the interplay of experience and things, an interplay that is necessarily but not disappointingly mysterious.

THE METHOD

Since the dawn of the modern era, philosophy has found itself in an increasingly embarrassing situation. The various sciences that philosophy has spun off have achieved independent success, happening upon a path of incremental progress, while philosophy itself seems unable to take a single step beyond its starting point. It is therefore science, not philosophy, that appears to hold the greatest promise for discovering ultimate truths. Yet science is not an oracle but a communion of inquirers, existing through time, committed to a general strategy for increasing our knowledge of the world through thoughtful experience. Since childhood we've been drilled in this method—observe, hypothesize, experiment. This approach constitutes a powerful way to widen our understanding of the natural world. Might we use the scientific method to examine experience itself?

At the heart of experience is the field of presence in which things can be encountered. You sit at home surrounded by ordinary things, including cups, couches, and television shows. You decide to visit the zoo and see exotic animals. On the way, you spot orange construction barrels, billboards, and traffic jams. At the zoo, you see hippos, chimps, and cheetahs. Through this day, many things have come to presence and receded into absence: couches, billboards, and hippos. This play of presence and absence is the essence of experience. Can there be a science of it? Can we observe presence as such? Not quite. We can observe that something, say, an elephant, is present, but we cannot observe presence. Why not? Because every observation requires presence as a necessary condition. We can observe gorilla behavior or electron behavior and we can observe someone observing gorillas and electrons but we cannot observe the field of presence that makes these observations possible; rather, presence is something we live through thanks to which we can have access to gorillas, electrons, and the people about us. Presence is not there to be observed in the way that gorillas, electrons, and other people are there to be observed. And if we cannot observe presence, that means we cannot hypothesize about it or run an experiment on it. Yet it does not turn out to be something nebulous and relative just because the method of modern natural science cannot get it into its grips. There's another equally rigorous method for getting a hold on experience, and it is this method that phenomenologists have carefully pioneered. In the place of science's triple command—observe, hypothesize, and experiment—phenomenology has its own triple: indicate, return, and explicate. This triple enacts the transcendental reduction, which is called "transcendental" because it has to do with the structure of experience, and "reduction" because it is a matter of leading back or returning to the latent sources of experience, sources that are always and everywhere operative although we do not attend to them as such.

1. *Indicate and Question*: Phenomenology leads with clues, words like *truth*, *experience*, and *time* that show up in everyday discourse but are inexplicable in terms of the horizon of that discourse. Augustine famously says, "What then is time? Provided that no one asks me, I know. If I want to explain it to an inquirer, I do not know."[1] Everyone knows what these words mean but it is very difficult to think about them. These elusive terms are signs that point us beyond observation to a more original layer of experience. Similarly, the philosophical tradition provides us suggestions for truths we might come to see for ourselves. We put a question mark next to these positions and then turn to see whether or not they express the way things are.

2. *Return*: Instead of observing what shows up in experience, we must return to the context in which things can show up. Unlike the indirect methods of science—methods

appropriate for getting at those things that show up *in* experience—phenomenology offers a direct method that gets right to experience itself. Hence there is no place for hypothesis and the indirect confirmation or disconfirmation of experiment. Instead, there is a direct exhibition of experience such that it is either successfully exhibited or not. Husserl writes,

> Because in the most impressive of the modern sciences, the mathematico-physical, that which is exteriorly the largest part of their work, results from indirect methods, we are only too inclined to overestimate indirect methods and to misunderstand the value of direct comprehensions. However, to the extent that philosophy goes back to ultimate origins, it belongs precisely to its very essence that its scientific work move in spheres of direct intuition.[2]

The point is a simple one. Indirect methods presuppose a direct access to experience; the method for getting at that direct access, accordingly, will need to be direct. Put differently, every causal model requires an experience as its basis, so that that experiential basis cannot itself be causally modeled. Instead, it needs to be directly exhibited. Phenomenology is this direct way of bringing us face to face, up close and personal, with the fundamental layer of experience, a layer presupposed by science and everyday life.

3. *Explicate*: Philosophy confronts us with fundamental experiential structures so that they might be articulated. It brings us back to phenomena not so that we may gape at them but so that we may let loose a language that makes explicit their implicit logic. Phenomenology recognizes an inner kinship between experience and language; the exhibited phenomena achieve a kind of completion when they are articulated. The challenge is to find a way of speaking that takes its bearings from the phenomena themselves and in this way lets them be exhibited and remembered as they are.

Indicate and Question

People can do biology for you and report the results. Little is lost on the reader for not having done the investigation. It is otherwise for phenomenology. To capture the nature of this situation, phenomenologists say that phenomenological terms are *indications*. That means that reading them passively will achieve for you precisely nothing. Instead, you have to read them actively, regarding them as invitations for investigations that must be performed by you and no one else in your stead. Only you can turn for yourself to the activity of experiencing that continually furnishes you with a world of experienced things. And all the terms that phenomenologists employ will be misunderstood if they are understood according to our usual way of thinking about experienced things. The function of an indication is not to inform (i.e., "This is what it's called") but to direct your search (i.e., "That is where it can be found").

Suppose you are on a walk through the woods, get lost, and are looking for a way out. You come across an arrow mounted on a tree with the words, "Main Campsite." You won't arrive at that campsite in virtue of reading the sign. Nor will you arrive at the campsite by ignoring the sign. You will arrive at the campsite by heeding the sign and heading in the direction it indicates. So it is with phenomenology. Phenomenological books are trail markers, which take on their proper sense only by those endeavoring to make the hike for themselves. Terms such as world, flesh, speech, truth, life, and love take on new meanings in a phenomenological context. The meanings of these words are attached to the phenomenological analyses that fill in their sense.

Heidegger specifies that ordinary terms can serve as *formal indications* for philosophical analyses.[3] He calls them "indications," because they cannot be understood in a straightforward way; their very meaning can be fixed only thanks to the successful completion of an investigation that must be undertaken individually. And he calls them "formal," because these indications direct us not to the content of experience but instead to the relational structure of experience. Phenomenology articulates the interconnected web of relations that constitute the field of experience, and it does so by formally indicating these relations one by one in a zigzag fashion. For example, Heidegger formally indicates the term "care." In ordinary discourse, the term is bound up with warm feelings of fellowship and kind actions. Heidegger's care, however, drills down deep to name the very structure of our experiential exploration of the world, a structure that accommodates itself to the things of this world, even as it perpetually raises the issue of its own good and the good of all those it encounters. Ordinary "care-talk" is not entirely misleading; it has some of the right associations. But it must be stretched and twisted beyond its own resources to name a basic phenomenological structure that makes experience possible. We experience things in virtue of care, a fundamental openness to things, others, and indeed our very selves.

It is not only everyday life in which we find directions for entering into phenomenology. Husserl sees the history of philosophy as a rich source of inspiration. It can become fruitful for us if we first distance ourselves from received accounts of the truth. We turn the claim into a question for our own research. He names this distancing using the Greek word *epoché*, meaning to suspend judgment.

> The *philosophical epoché* that we adopt should, to
> put it formally, consist in the fact that we *completely*

withhold judgment regarding the doctrinal content
of all previous philosophy and carry out all our
demonstrations within the framework of withholding
such judgment.[4]

We'll not accept as true anything that has been said in the history of philosophy itself unless we can see it's true for ourselves, and then we won't accept it because it is said but because it is true. Phenomenology's motto, to return from words and theories to the things themselves, suggests that we should understand the history of philosophy as offering so many suggestions for research.

Heidegger develops this relationship to the tradition and argues that phenomenology can make progress only by dismantling the philosophical tradition. Now, it is easier to destroy than to build, but it is very difficult to reverse engineer something, to take it apart so that you can understand how it was made. To reverse engineer requires figuring out how someone else thought about something; it means getting into the mind of another insofar as that mind is on display in what was made. It is supremely difficult work. But in doing it, one's horizons become widened, deepened. One sees more, one sees a way forward; one figures out how something has been done and is thereby afforded the possibility of doing something just as well and often better. Heidegger pioneers the idea of reverse engineering previous philosophies in order to find the living truth those philosophers saw and to express that more originally for ourselves.

One might object that the idea of dismantling seems negative. The answer is that it is profoundly positive. It views the history of philosophy as a fecund source of suggestions for how the world is; only by returning to these claims and reanimating them for ourselves will we be in a position to judge their truth.

> Construction in philosophy is necessarily destruction, that is to say, a de-constructing of traditional concepts carried out in a historical recursion to the tradition. And this is not a negation of the tradition or a condemnation of it as worthless; quite the reverse, it signifies a positive appropriation of tradition.[5]

Any philosopher wants to be read not as an authority but as a witness; the very sense of philosophy is to go beyond the philosopher to the world the philosopher seeks to understand.

Heidegger's method of dismantling is a way of taking seriously the nature of philosophy as a collaborative activity involving inevitable missteps. We cannot get things exactly right all the time, but in attending to others' attempts to get things exactly right, we can get more things right than we otherwise would.

Heidegger says that he thought to articulate the structure of the field of experience in terms of care only because of Augustine's central use of the term.[6] In the *Confessions*, Augustine says that he was entrusted with the task of bringing about a kind of unity to his life through care; and he also details certain tendencies that must be continually resisted in order to maintain this unity before God.[7] Heidegger finds this invocation of care and the dynamics of experience richly suggestive, and he retrieves them in his own voice, endeavoring to bring to expression the unity of the phenomenological domain. He does not merely repeat them, but goes back to the phenomenon and says something new in light of them. What for Augustine was the soul's transcendence of the world toward God became re-described by Heidegger as the self's transcendence of things toward its own greatest possibility for being.

Heidegger observes that phenomenology is necessary, because we do not ordinarily experience things as they are. Why not? Because we remain bound to superficial interpretations that people make. Heidegger says that "we do not say what we see, but rather the reverse, we see what *one says* about the matter."[8] All too easily we parrot the viewpoints we pick up in the media rather than take the trouble to arrive at the truth of the matter. Husserl thinks this "seduction of language" promotes a purely associative thinking that is refuted by new experience.[9] The epoché converts these often-heard opinions about things into suggestions. The phenomenological task is to return to the things themselves and to thereby have the position confirmed or corrected. Phenomenology begins by putting quotation marks about traditional views, and it ends by removing them if it can.[10] It is not a matter of doubting but of renewing. Phenomenology brings insights back to life by reexperiencing the truth of their inception.

Why bother with the tradition at all? Why not just make a clean start? Phenomenology gambles that the basic terms and posture of the tradition can help guide us toward truth. It trusts that the tradition is worth our while, and again and again, this confidence bears fruit.[11] The insights of a Plato or Aristotle, or an Augustine or Kant, come suddenly to life again through phenomenological research. Instead of positions that might be summarized in an encyclopedia article or memorized by wary undergraduates, these claims become invested with a power to express the wondrous truth of things; they become compelling in their articulation of what is. Grappling with the tradition thereby gives us the opportunity to register the inveterate prejudices of our own time and provokes us to see more of the inexhaustible field of experience. Of course, much of what philosophers have said must be left behind, but much remains that can become illuminating again.

Phenomenology brings insights back to life by reexperiencing the truth of their inception.

Return

Suppose you are running late when traffic snarls. Normally, that experience draws us in so that we mutter expletives under our breath and curse our luck. Our focus remains squarely on the aspects of the situation: the stopped cars, the impending appointment, our own routine failure to allot enough time before appointments to cope with such jams, and so on. But note that in order for all these features of the situation to be there, they have to be experienced by us: we perceive, we make sense of the problem, we feel frustration, and so on. It remains possible, while still undergoing the experience, to shift registers and to attend to the experiencing itself rather than the experienced. Now what is experienced exercises a pull on us but we can deliberately resist that pull and retreat toward the horizon of the experiencing itself: What is it to perceive the traffic jam; what is it to understand the red lights and turn signals of the stop-and-go traffic; what is it to feel the keen frustration of the whole affair; what is it, moreover, to be one who can undergo and achieve all these sorts of experiences? To ask these questions is to make a turn, the transcendental turn, from what is experienced to the activity of experience.

By inviting us to make this shift, phenomenology wants to make a fundamental clarification. In order to follow phenomenology we have to lay aside again the temptation that inserts itself at just this juncture. When we make this turn to experience we are liable to think that our goal is to construct a model of how experience occurs; after all, models are a typical way in which we seek to elevate what we experience into the realm of knowledge. Phenomenology, however, bucks against this pressure and issues a warning that in this context making a model would be a fatal blunder. We make models only for those things that we cannot experience directly. We make a model of the motion of the planets about the sun, because, being on one of those planets, we lack the ideal vantage point, somewhere above the solar system, to see how the various planets follow elliptical orbits about the sun. We make a model of the smearing movement of electrons around their nucleus, because we have only indirect experience of things that small. But the activity that makes experience possible is, after all, something that is experienced. We don't have to deduce it, infer it, or model it. We can directly exhibit it. As we go about the world, we are engrossed in things and our projects. We can use things, build things, or study things. But we can also return to the context in which all these activities are possible. The default mode of ordinary, everyday existence, the one engrossed in things and projects, is called the *natural* or *everyday attitude*. And it is not so much an attitude, which suggests an artificial bearing, but the way in which things ordinarily show up in our experience. On the margins of this mode of experience is another mode, the *philosophical attitude*. Here I follow up the instigations of wonder, I deliberately turn to the margins of ordinary experience, and I become practiced in a new mode of experience—a mode trained not on things and projects but on experience itself. I thereby enter the transcendental reduction to arrive at phenomenology proper.

Heidegger adopts Husserl's idea of the natural attitude but not its verbiage, since he thinks there's nothing particularly natural about ignoring presence and there is nothing artificial or unnatural in paying attention to it, and because the very idea of attitude, even in the technical philosophical sense meant by Husserl, implies a kind of approach to things that is not at all ordinary. Heidegger instead wants us to see that our default mode of approach is to be immersed in things, focused on things, and therefore negligent of their presence. Heidegger offers phenomenology as a disruption of the default, a going against the grain of experience to shift from things to their presence. "We have to look around in factical life experience in order to obtain a motive for its turning around."[12]

In the philosophical attitude I attend not simply to things and projects but to how things and projects are accessible to experience. I do not ask *whether* things are accessible; I am not doubting their availability. I do not try to substitute an artificial bridge to things for the natural bridge inherent in experience. Rather, I attend to *how* things are accessible, *how* they arise in the field of experience. The different modalities of experience now come in for explicit investigation. The structures of the field, structures always there in affording me things, call out for explication.

In this dazzling new mode of experience, a new world opens up, new not in the sense that it is being created by my gaze, but new in the sense that what has always been there but was not minded by me as such is now explicitly there before me. The act of returning spurred by wonder and chosen by me affords an unlimited number of explorations. It is a new field of research, a new area for investigation. This land is our birthright, and we do well to return to it, cultivate it, and let it bear fruit. For the field of experience, when rejuvenated, will renew our appreciation for all those things and projects that show up within it.

We do well to care about care and thereby to come back to ourselves and our experience of things with a renewed intensity. Heidegger aims to motivate this caring about care by means of what he calls fundamental moods, such as wonder, joy, and profound boredom. The mood he most discusses is anxiety, which he distinguishes sharply from any sort of psychological state. Phenomenology's interest lies in the fact that anxiety brings us face to face with care. Something like fear is always fear before something, whether a particular something—*this* bear—or a general object of worry—*vicious animals*. But anxiety is different from fear because it is not an aversion to this, that, or the other thing. Heidegger invites us to see in the occasional occurrence of this sort of anxiety a worry that worries about having to worry, a revelation of the fundamental relational structure of experience. *"That in the face of which one has anxiety is being-in-the-world as such."*[13] In our very being we are primed to care for things, ourselves, and each other. We can do this badly or well; that's our choice—but what isn't our choice is the fact of our caring. Something like anxiety or joy in the presence of a loved one lets us catch sight of care; the experience helps move us from an empty indication, a mere word sound, "care," toward the reality of the phenomenon, and it thereby readies us to unpack its intelligibility.

Explication

As we saw in the last chapter, eidetic intuition is a way of getting at the natures of things, of bringing the ideas of things to explicit awareness. It allows us to grasp what things are in three directions: first, and most obviously, everyday things and topics, such as the nature of love and justice or democratic leadership; second, the different modes of experience, such as the difference between memory and perception or imagination and anticipation; third, the transcendental correlation of experience and things.[14]

In this way, phenomenology clarifies the thoughtful ability to grasp the essence of something, but it also applies this clarified ability to what it alone enables us to have access to, namely, the field of experience as such.

Thanks to the return the field is laid bare. Hence it becomes possible for phenomenology to research the essential features of the field. What does it find? The very topics of this book: there is *world* as the place of experience; *flesh* as the embodied agency of different points of view in that field; *speech* as a way of manifesting things in that field or of talking about that field itself; *truth* as the givenness of something in that field just as it is manifested in speech; *life* as the task of dwelling in openness to truth; *love* as the explicit sharing of this field with another; *wonder* as the becoming attentive to the field as such. The various analyses in the foregoing chapters amount to various initial explications of this very fertile field of presence. However, these analyses comprise only a sample of the phenomena of chief interest to phenomenologists as they research the structures of presence. There are phenomenological investigations of time and space as that which affords presence as well as investigations of such phenomena as the genesis of logic, mathematics, and science from out of the lifeworld of shared experience.

Heidegger characterizes care as follows: "the being of human existence means ahead-of-itself-being-already-in-(the-world) as being-near (entities encountered within-the-world)."[15] There's no easy path to understanding what this means. The terms formally indicate a direction of investigation that concerns not things in their particular content but rather our relation to them. Heidegger deploys the hyphen in great abundance to capture something of the web of relations that constitute our domain of experience. His formula not only bids us to turn to this domain but also endeavors to explicate it, to articulate it, to bring it to linguistic expression. He names three elements that he welds together. First, human experience is "ahead of itself"; that is, it goes beyond itself in view of its interests. Second, human experience is "already in the world"; that is, experience takes place in a shared context rather than in our own heads. Third, by virtue of our going beyond in a shared world, we can "be near" things we encounter. Heidegger's care names the very way things can come to presence thanks to our active exploration of the shared world.

The threefold structure of care finds support in the threefold structure of time. We stretch out beyond things in terms of care for ourselves and others. We plan and put these plans into action. In this way we exist toward the future. But all these projects take their bearing from the fact that we already find ourselves in a particular situation in which a host of things are given. In this way our open futural existence is delimited by what has already been. In light of our forward movement that is determined by the past, we can then make things present as the very things they are; in stretching out beyond things we run up against them in their otherness.

The triple movement of indication, return, and explication harbors within itself a hidden power to unlock the unfathomed depths of experience thanks to which each of us shares a world of things. The foregoing chapters made silent use of this method. In this way they impart something of the fruitfulness of phenomenology's investigations of the essence of experience. As spectators to experience, we have the task of registering the truth of the structures of the experiential world. Phenomenology's transcendental reduction leads us into an explicit possession of the terms—world, flesh, speech, truth, life, love, and wonder—that put us into touch with the things themselves.

THE MOVEMENT

Husserl envisions a joint venture of thousands of collaborating phenomenological researchers, and Heidegger describes research as a renewal of life itself. At the same time, the collaborative renewal often succumbs, like much of human affairs, to falling-outs and dead ends. Hence it is often anything but what it aims to be. This chapter maps and assuages conflicts arising regarding the phenomenological movement. All these conflicts are overblown; they are rooted principally in misunderstandings and differences in emphasis.[1] Heidegger is, from start to finish, thoroughly phenomenological, and other movements in what is called "continental philosophy" are intelligible only to the extent that they retain the phenomenology of truth. At its heart phenomenology remains a collaborative venture of researchers renewing the very movement of experience. The rallying cry, "Back to the things themselves," has lost none of its allure as it invites all of us to recover the richness of experience.

Advent (1900)

Edmund Husserl (1859–1938) was a mathematician who, in trying to make sense of the origin of number and truth in mathematics, became one of the most original and influential philosophers of the last two centuries. His breakthrough work, the *Logical Investigations* (1900–1901), demonstrates that empirical accounts of truth are self-defeating and then examines nonetheless just how truth can arise in experience without being reducible to that experience: How can contingent experience access necessary truths? How did we, for example, arrive at the experience that confirms the fact that $2 + 2 = 4$? To make sense of this, he must insist that there is more to experience than subjective impression; subjectivity, rightly understood, carries objective import. To be faithful to the original experience of truth, he advocates widening intuition from mere sensible qualities to categorial relations. I don't see just bits of color and flashes of light that I internally work up into a model of a cat and a mat; I can look out into the world and see the cat's being on the mat. The state of affairs, made present to me through my action, presents itself to me in the flesh so that I can see and register its truth. With such a rich account of experience as open to the truth of things, Husserl offers something that many philosophers want. Here we have a new way of philosophizing that claims we can bring about a direct exhibition of what we are talking about; instead of theories at war with one another, Husserl maps a way for philosophical peace by retreating from the battlefield of thought and returning to the field of experience, which alone can and should be called on to settle such disputes.

Despite the broad appeal of his method, Husserl ends up starting a movement that lacks disciples of the strict observance. Each phenomenologist takes up phenomenology only to question something in the master's ideas and to press further into the things themselves. To his credit, Husserl develops a movement that isn't about Husserl, isn't about fidelity to Husserlian doctrines, but is instead a liberating quest to come to terms with the truth of things, a quest in which nothing is sacrosanct, not even the positions adopted by its founder. It might seem like a failure on Husserl's part that he did not inspire devotees (indeed, it was a source of bitter disappointment and feelings of betrayal for him), but it is in fact a mark of his success as a philosopher that he didn't. Max Scheler saw this early and clearly:

There is no phenomenological "school" which would have to offer commonly accepted theses. There is only a circle of researchers, inspired by a common bearing and attitude toward philosophical problems, who take and bear separate responsibility for everything they claim to have discovered within this attitude, including any theory of the nature of this "attitude."[2]

Phenomenology is no ideology, no system, no finished product there for the taking. It is rather something alive and growing, adapting to different considerations, aspiring ever to fulfill the mandate to return to the things themselves. Husserl planted a seed prone to mutate with each generation, and many of these mutations serve only to make phenomenology more vigorous and plentiful depending on the surrounding environment.

The Question of the Transcendental Turn (1913)

Many of Husserl's contemporaries accused him of a contradiction in his breakthrough work. How, they asked him, can you maintain both that truth is not something empirical and that truth arises in experience? Husserl realizes that to make truth into something merely empirical is to make it into something relative, and he realizes that to separate truth from experience is to remain closed to the very way in which we arrive at the truths that we seek to defend. Husserl's solution, first published in *Ideas I* (1913), is to make the transcendental turn. Experience can access truths that transcend experience, because there's a fundamental difference between empirical experience and transcendental experience. Empirical experience deals with the contingent features of experience; transcendental experience brings to experience the unvarying structures at play in experience. Some of his followers who had enthusiastically greeted his breakthrough work turn their noses at this new development. How could Husserl abandon realism for modern idealism? Students such as Roman Ingarden (1893–1970) and Dietrich von Hildebrand (1889–1977) think that Husserl, instead of returning to the things themselves, gets entangled in ideas. In this way, Husserl betrays phenomenology, substituting dogma for experience. Is this right? Does Husserl sell out?

In Husserl's own mind, his turn is not a betrayal; rather, it has the single aim of saving the return to the things themselves. Husserl bemoans "the extraordinarily widespread inclination of our times *to psychologize the eidetic*," that is, to think that essences are somehow nothing more than "mental constructs."[3] He thinks that it is only by making this transcendental turn that one can save the essences of things. Near the end of his life, he looks back on his thought and affirms the inner connection between the *Logical Investigations* and the turn of the *Ideas*:

The first breakthrough of this universal a priori of correlation between experienced object and manners of givenness (which occurred during work on my *Logical Investigations* around 1898) affected me so deeply that my whole subsequent life-work has been dominated by the task of systematically elaborating on this a priori of correlation. The further course of the reflections in this text will show how, when human subjectivity was brought into the problems of correlation, a radical transformation of the meaning of these problems became necessary which finally led to the phenomenological reduction to absolute, transcendental subjectivity.[4]

At least in Husserl's own understanding, then, not only is there no break between *Logical Investigations* and the *Ideas*; the *Ideas* are the necessary elaboration of the return to the things themselves accomplished by the *Logical Investigations*. If we can return to the things themselves, it is in virtue of our radical openness to the truth of things. Now, in working out this openness, it is true that Husserl adopts more of the lingo from German Idealism than is helpful, and this language erects unnecessary obstacles to phenomenology's reception. But his later clarity regarding the method of transcendental reduction does not compromise the reality of things and essences; rather, it safeguards them by recognizing that experiencing something is other than making; experiencing is not a causal trans-action that would thereby make the experienced thing or essence into an artifact of experience. Realism without the transcendental turn destroys the reality of essences. That, after all, was Nietzsche's pre-phenomenological mis-take. Experience is not essentially a causal occurrence; it is, instead, a matter of allowing something to come to light as it is in itself. Husserl's transcendental turn, far from compromising the truth that essences and things have an independence vis-à-vis experience, in fact safeguards that truth and exists for no other reason.

The most original of Husserl's early collaborators is the larger-than-life, intuitive personality Max Scheler (1874–1928), who deploys phenomenology to investigate the structures of love and value. What Husserl accom-plishes in the area of logic, mapping the contours of ex-perience as its basis, Scheler accomplishes in the area of ethics. His attention to the heart is a crucial bridge for un-derstanding how Husserl's orientation to logic shifts into Heidegger's focus on the human and its openness to being.

Husserl and Heidegger (1927)

From a crop of highly talented students, Husserl hand-picks as his successor Martin Heidegger (1889–1976), who is brilliant, obscure, and deeply troubling. At first, this seems to be a happy arrangement. In 1927, Heidegger dedicates his magnum opus, *Being and Time*, to Husserl, and he explains his indebtedness to him:

> But to disclose the *a priori* is not to make an "*a-prioristic*" construction. Edmund Husserl has not only enabled us to understand once more the meaning of any genuine philosophical "empiricism"; he has also given us the necessary tools.[5]

While the Neo-Kantians endeavored to makes an indirect model of experience, phenomenology instead shows us how to bring experience directly to experience. It is in this way that phenomenology can be considered the first genuinely philosophical empiricism. And yet, in short order, the subterranean rift between the founder and his successor becomes apparent, and there occurs a famous falling-out of disastrous consequences for the phenomenological movement. In his copy of Heidegger's *Being and Time*, Husserl writes: *amicus Plato magis amica veritas*, "Plato is a friend, truth a greater friend."[6] Husserl here echoes Aristotle's famous comment that though Plato was his teacher and friend, he had to disagree with him wherever he got something wrong. Similarly, Husserl and Heidegger, heretofore friends, disagree over the truth, which has a greater claim to their allegiance than each other. What happened? How did the twin giants of phenomenology end up turning against one another? The disagreement has to do with the human being and its relation to the truth of experience.

Husserl's basic charge is that Heidegger relates everything to human existence with *disastrous* results:

> Heidegger transposes or changes the constitutive-phenomenological clarification of all regions of entities and universals, of the total region of the world, into the anthropological: the whole problematic is shifted over: corresponding to the ego there is human existence, etc. In that way everything becomes ponderously unclear, and philosophically loses its value.[7]

Husserl thereby gives Heidegger's *Being and Time* an "F," and he says just about the worst thing about it you can say about a work of philosophy: it is obscure and worthless. Is Husserl right? What Husserl cannot see is that Heidegger's aim is not to reduce the truth of experience to the anthropological; it is to come up with a new understanding of the human in terms of the experience of truth. As Heidegger puts it in a letter to Husserl in 1927:

> We are in agreement on the fact that entities in the sense of what you call "world" cannot be explained in their transcendental constitution by returning to an entity of the same mode of being.

But that does not mean that what makes up the place of the transcendental is not an entity at all; rather, precisely at this juncture there arises the *problem*: What is the mode of being of the entity in which "world" is constituted? That is *Being and Time*'s central problem—namely, a fundamental ontology of human existence. It has to be shown that the mode of being of human existence is totally different from that of all other entities and that, as the mode of being that it is, it harbors right within itself the possibility of transcendental constitution.[8]

Who experiences experience? Each one of us, of course. To name us *as recipients of experience*, Husserl calls us "transcendental egos"—"transcendental," because it concerns the possibility of experience, and "egos," because it concerns each of us. We are not only those for whom experience happens; we also are those who show up in experience. Suppose you are sitting on your back porch drinking iced tea on a sizzling hot day. You experience the waves of warmth across your whole body and experience the stinging temperature of the ice-cold beverage. Glancing at your hand, you see the condensation drip down from the glass to land on your knee. In this experience, you are there not only as the recipient of the experience, but you also show up as one of the things experienced. Your knee, pelted by drips of water, is one of the things that appears in the world of your experience alongside the hot day, the glass of iced tea, and the like. Husserl calls that part of us that shows up in experience the "empirical ego," the self as experienced. Husserl, then, gives us two terms for the one person: the transcendental ego that experiences the world and the empirical ego that is experienced in that world.

Heidegger agrees with the general Husserlian strategy of noting how different it is to regard the self as the recipient of experience and to regard the self as one that shows up in that experience, but, beyond Husserl, he wants to emphasize that the self is one and the same across this radical divide. How can there be one and the same self that is both the agent of experience and one that is experienced, both the transcendental and empirical egos? Heidegger coins a term to name this unified, bimodal self, or, better, he presses an ordinary philosophical term into new service. He calls the unified human being "Dasein." At this point many translators give up and it is therefore commonplace to find this German term strewn through English translations of Heidegger's prose, but this is hardly helpful for the English-speaking reader. Dasein is the German word for "existence," and Heidegger uses it to refer to the essence of human beings as experiencers of truth. Hence I find it illuminating to render Dasein in English as "human existence."[9] Heidegger confronts the divide in the self between that which experiences and that which is experienced, between the one who takes experience in and the one that shows up in that field as one being among many. Human existence is capable, Heidegger wants us to see, of a radical and free shift, in which we register ourselves not only as one thing among many but as the one that is the nodal point of experience. Human existence names that unique way of being that embraces both the transcendental and empirical egos.

Husserl finds phenomenological forerunners in Kant, Descartes, and Augustine, and Heidegger in Kant, Augustine, and Aristotle. For Heidegger, phenomenology's novelty is the recovery of the original mode of philosophizing at work in the Greek experience of things. For Husserl, phenomenology for the first time makes explicit the methodological requirements of experience. He writes that "phenomenology is, as it were, the secret longing of all modern philosophy."[10] For Husserl, then, phenomenology constitutes the *fulfillment* of philosophy, especially in its modern quest to clarify experience; for Heidegger, phenomenology constitutes a *rediscovery* of philosophy and its quest to experience the intelligibility of things. In neither case is phenomenology something without precedent in the history of philosophy. In light of the contemporary worked-out conception of philosophy, it then becomes possible to read the history of philosophy phenomenologically.

In the last decade of his life, Husserl presents two new introductions to his philosophy, *Cartesian Meditations* and *The Crisis*. In the former, he takes over the Cartesian mode of questioning and repurposes it for phenomenology; in the latter, he distinguishes phenomenology from psychology and presents phenomenology as the solution to the antagonisms between life and knowledge that plague modernity. Husserl's most engaging writings come from this fertile period, and he also publishes two studies on the origin of logic in experience: *Formal and Transcendental Logic* and *Experience and Judgment*.

Analytic Philosophy (1932)

In 1929, Heidegger takes over Husserl's chair in Freiburg. He delivers an infamous inaugural lecture, "What Is Metaphysics?" In it, he deploys an over-the-top rhetorical device to provoke the gathered scientists to reflect on the ground of the sciences in philosophical inquiry. He says that phenomenology, in contrast to all the sciences, studies "nothing." The idea, familiar to any reader of his *Being and Time*, is that experience takes place within a domain that is not a thing. This might sound strange, but consider an analogy: the written words on this page are different from the page itself. The writer who can't write, but finds the blank piece of paper or the dreaded blinking cursor on a blank screen staring back, experiences dread or angst before the pure possibility of writing. How can we speak of this blankness? It becomes tricky. Some books use the text "This page intentionally left blank." The problem is that in order to express the blankness, they've destroyed the blankness; there is now a sentence on the page! Heidegger's problem is analogous; he wants to call attention to the pure possibility of experience, the pure field of experience, and he wants to come up with an appropriate way of speaking about it without betraying its essence. Heidegger later likens it to happening upon a clearing: "If we stand in a clearing in the woods, we see only what can be found within it: the free place, the trees about—and precisely not the luminosity of the clearing itself."[11] Ordinarily, we overlook the place and the happening of experience for the things it affords us; phenomenology must work against this ordinary tendency.

Rudolf Carnap (1891–1970), a member of the Vienna Circle of logical positivists, finds the lecture's talk about the nothing to be positively infuriating. In his 1932 essay, "The Elimination of Metaphysics through Logical Analysis of Language," he singles it out as "Exhibit A" for the kind of pseudo-statements metaphysicians routinely make.[12] Carnap does not seem to realize that Heidegger is introducing not only a new way of talking; he is introducing a new kind of phenomenon and a new way of experiencing it. Now there is some agreement between Carnap and Heidegger; both are attentive to the role of experience in justifying philosophical claims. So the difference really turns on the question of whether experience is necessarily limited to things or whether it is possible to experience experience itself. Carnap's criticism amounts to this: "Only things can be experienced, and therefore all meaningful statements concern things. Now Heidegger says that the field of experience is not a thing. Heidegger's claim is therefore meaningless." The phenomenological rejoinder amounts to this: "Not all meaningful statements concern things, for the field of experience can be experienced and it is not a thing. The field of experience can therefore be meaningfully discussed." The debate turns, then, on whether there is an experience of experience, and that's a question for phenomenology, not logical analysis.

Today among professional philosophers, there are two rival camps. On the one side are those who belong to what is called "analytic philosophy" and are sympathetic to Carnap-style worries about philosophical excess; on the other are those who belong to continental philosophy (phenomenology) and are sympathetic to Heidegger-style questions about the relation of philosophy to science as well as the experience of truth. Analytic philosophers are supposed to be clear but pedestrian, and phenomenological authors are supposed to be obscure but profound. There is no doubt some element of truth in these caricatures, but they are of limited value. It is better to think of them as complementary, mutually enriching approaches to the field of philosophical inquiry. Analytic thought fosters critical thinking, the art of evaluating arguments and concepts for their coherence; phenomenology fosters perceptive thinking, the art of experiencing and analyzing the part–whole structures of things, essences, premises, and experience itself. Phenomenological authors who take analytic thought seriously tend to have an added approachability, and analytic authors who take phenomenology seriously tend to have an added richness. Phenomenology offers analysts a robust sense of experience that doesn't devolve into the irrelevance of the merely subjective, empirical, or contingent. Analytic philosophy offers phenomenologists a conceptual rigor that doesn't devolve into the merely clever or poetic.

Conceptual analysis and phenomenological elucidation are two tools that every philosopher does well to have on hand. Husserl regards these tools as complementary.[13] And Heidegger writes, "In our case, however, it is not a matter of deducing propositions and propositional sequences from one another, but of working out the access to the matters from which propositions are to be drawn to begin with."[14] Phenomenology is a way of philosophizing that carries us to the roots of arguments in essential experience.

Heidegger against Heidegger (1933)

Husserl was a Jew who converted to Christianity as a young man. Heidegger was a Catholic who became a

Phenomenology is a way of philosophizing that carries us to the roots of arguments in essential experience.

Protestant soon after marrying one. The National Socialists regarded phenomenology as a Jewish movement due to Husserl's roots. When they come to power, Heidegger disastrously saw them as holding the promise to renew European civilization, and he became the first Nazi rector of his university, a post he held for nine months. Much ink has been spilled and will continue to be spilled over this inexcusable episode in Heidegger's life.[15] The philosophical spirit should make one immune to nationalism and racial prejudice, and yet Heidegger clearly succumbs to the virus of ideology. What sense, if any, can be made of this? The important thing in this context is to see that Heidegger's sins have nothing to do with phenomenology; they remain Heidegger's own. He criticizes the *ordo amoris* in Scheler, missing its sure phenomenological foundation, and he suffers the penalty for it: to fall prey to nationalism reflects a clear idolatry and inversion of love. Another phenomenologist, Dietrich von Hildebrand, a student of Husserl, fights against National Socialism and as a result has to flee Germany to save his life.[16] We can distinguish Heidegger the man from Heidegger the phenomenologist. In fact, many of Heidegger's most talented students and followers were Jewish. Among these were Hannah Arendt (1906–1975), Leo Strauss (1899–1973), Hans Jonas (1903–1993), and Emmanuel Lévinas (1906–1995). They could see the value of the philosophy despite the scandal and embarrassment of the philosopher's life.

Metaphysics (1935)

Phenomenology is an account of experience, which defends our ability to apprehend the essence and truth of things. Does this topic and task exhaust philosophy? In particular, does it foreclose the possibility of metaphysics, which inquires into the essence and existence of things in themselves? Husserl typically ends his introductions with a gesture toward metaphysics. Heidegger originally sees phenomenology as nothing other than an inquiry into the groundwork for metaphysics. But beginning around 1935, he distances his inquiry from metaphysics, and even comes to speak of his thought as transcending metaphysics. Does Heidegger in the end follow Carnap in thinking that metaphysics is impossible?

Heidegger comes to think that the metaphysical tradition does a poor job of explaining experience; it always explains experience as the relation between one thing and another and thereby overlooks the phenomenon of world. But to say that metaphysics does a poor job of answering phenomenology's question is different from saying it does a poor job of answering its own question about the being of things.

Phenomenology's great discovery is to work out how experience does not dilute the independence of things from experience but instead allows us to know them in their independence. Back to the things themselves means that we have returned to those selfsame transcendent things. What about these essences that experience constitutes but does not fabricate? What about the existence of things that experience runs up against? Why are things the way they are? Why do things exist at all? And why do we exist, those for whom experience happens? Even after we've explained the givenness of experience in terms of the presencing and absencing of time and history, we still have not explained the givenness of the existence of things, the fact that they are as they are. Husserl observes,

> As phenomenologists we also execute positings, actual theoretical position-takings, but they are exclusively directed toward lived-processes and lived-process correlates. In ontology, on the other hand, we perform actual positings that are directed toward the objects pure and simple, instead of toward the correlates and objects in quotation marks.[17]

Something does not cease to be because it is absent; nor is it present solely in virtue of existing. The play of presence and absence is other than the play of existence and nonexistence. There's thus more to wonder than phenomenology explores. The metaphysical inquiry into the transcendence of essence and the causality of existence remains a real possibility, which complements rather than competes with phenomenology.

Existential Phenomenology (1943)

In 1929, Husserl travels to France to give the Paris Lectures; as a result, the phenomenological movement gains traction and new life there. Gabriel Marcel (1889–1973), who coined the term "existentialism," is broadly phenomenological in his outlook, and he develops a phenomenological account of everyday life in the contemporary world, focusing especially on the interplay of alienation and participation and the importance of the living body. The great French phenomenologist Maurice Merleau-Ponty (1901–1961), whose *Phenomenology of Perception* remains a classic, deploys considerable energies to talk about the triple, self–other–thing, as it is at play in the work of perceptual experience; in dialogue with psychology, he points out the essential structures in perception and how a shared world arises thanks to our individual resources. Jean-Paul Sartre (1905–1980) and Simone de Beauvoir (1908–1996) embrace the mantra of existentialism but often do so at the expense of a phenomenological commitment to experience as the domain of truth; the result is an emphasis on freedom that verges on caprice. For Sartre, we are "condemned to be free."[18] In the spiritual wasteland that opened after the Second World War, their existentialism overshadows phenomenology in providing Stoic counsel to be responsible for oneself and one's own emotions. Existentialism's brute freedom is a phenomenological mistake. In reality, freedom finds itself within the compass of a horizon of truths highlighted by love.

The Early and the Late Heidegger (1947)

The single most influential text in twentieth-century philosophy remains unfinished. At first, Heidegger's *Being and Time* is too big to fit into Husserl's yearbook as a whole, so the final systematic section and the entire second half on the history of philosophy are left out when it is published in 1927. Then Heidegger grows dissatisfied with the draft of that section, and he attempts to rewrite it for imminent publication. Finally, Heidegger abandons all hope of finishing the text according to the plan he had laid down, and he decides he needs to make a fresh start. As a result, *Being and Time* will remain, for all eternity, incomplete. What is the relation between Heidegger's magnum opus and his later writings? It is only in *Being and Time* that he completely identifies himself with phenomenology; in his later writings, which first begin to be published in 1947, the term drops away, and he describes what he does as *thinking* rather than as *phenomenology*. Did Heidegger abandon phenomenology?

A careful review of his principles reveals that everything that he prizes about phenomenology in 1927 remains prized by him in his later thinking, and in fact he makes the shift he does in an attempt to be even more phenomenological than he had been in *Being and Time*. In a famous passage in which Heidegger explains why he could not finish his magnum opus, he writes,

> In the poverty of its first breakthrough, the thinking that tries to advance thought into the truth of being brings only a small part of that wholly other dimension to language. This language even falsifies itself for it does not yet succeed in retaining the essential help of phenomenological seeing while dispensing with the inappropriate concern with "science" and "research."[19]

He wishes to be an even more effective phenomenologist, to bring even more of the phenomenological domain to experience and expression. It is not phenomenological experience that he is jettisoning. Rather, he is attempting to find a vocabulary that will more adequately express the "letting show itself" at work in phenomenological experience.[20] The so-called later Heidegger does not waiver in his commitment to phenomenology, waiver in his commitment to "the letting show itself of the proper matter of thought."[21] He rather remains thoroughly phenomenological from start to finish, wavering only in the style of language he presses to serve his phenomenological purposes.

His technical vocabulary yields to a more poetic form of expression, and it does so simply because he thinks the poetic form more ably expresses the experience of experience that is phenomenology.

Hermeneutics (1960)

In *Being and Time*, Heidegger calls his version of phenomenology "hermeneutic" in a subtle development of Husserl's method. Hermeneutics is a term that originally concerns the difficulty of making sense of a text, especially the Bible. In applying it to phenomenology, Heidegger wishes to highlight the constitutive role of understanding and interpretation in the logic of experience. Things are experienced by us *as* something or another. In Germany, Heidegger's student Hans-Georg Gadamer (1900–2002) develops a rich account of making sense of texts and all experience under the banner of "hermeneutics," all the while continuing to practice the art of phenomenological seeing. In France, Paul Ricoeur (1913–2005), a brilliantly original phenomenologist, likewise takes to characterizing his work as hermeneutics. It might seem that hermeneutics has a kind of independence vis-à-vis phenomenology, but in fact interpretation is but a moment of phenomenological explication; hermeneutics aims to show how truth arises within the experience of interpretation. Gadamer famously speaks of a "fusion of horizons," which is a way of naming the phenomenological experience of world at play in making sense of the work of another.[22] To read Plato's *Republic*, for example, is a matter of trying to re-animate the sense of the world of experience that reverberates in and through it. Gadamer and Ricoeur, as well as their progeny, constitute an application of phenomenological analysis to textual wholes and conversation. In this way, hermeneutics belongs to the phenomenological task of elucidating the experience of truth.

Postmodernism (1967)

It is obligatory to say something of the one-time phenomenological commentator, Jacques Derrida (1930–2004), whose clever and often insightful readings of Husserl and other figures in the history of philosophy garnered much attention in the final decades of the twentieth century. Derrida draws from Heidegger's focus on that dimension of experience that always escapes us, and he reads all philosophical texts in light of some key idea that ever eludes the thinker, some central notion that just can't be pinned down. Derrida inspires many devotees, especially outside philosophy in literary studies; his invention of deconstruction seems to be a method that works against the phenomenological quest to return to the things themselves.

Instead, he wants to show that the philosophical quest is doomed to fail; the things will always escape us; our nets will always come up empty.

In reality, to the degree to which deconstruction makes sense, it is but a part of the phenomenological method. As I mentioned in chapter 9, Heidegger pioneers a way of reading the philosophical tradition in terms of reverse engineering what philosophers have said in order to discover the original experiences that prompt these formulations. Heidegger does so in order to free us up to elucidate the phenomenon in our own voice. Derrida isolates the negative moment, the destruction, and he takes it out of the positive movement toward the phenomenon; in doing so, he undercuts its motive and renders the exercise pointless. Why pick apart except to clear the way to see afresh?

Postmodern thinkers such as Michel Foucault (1926–1984) question the adequacy of phenomenology's first-person perspective. After all, we remain determined by historical forces that we cannot bring to intuitive givenness except through the detour of a third-person historical register. Foucault turns to examples such as madness and sexuality to demonstrate that the current understanding of these things changes from era to era, and these understandings in turn affect how individuals experience themselves. What we regard as a mental illness to be isolated was at one time an aberration to be celebrated. Foucault believes that the flux of such historical realities means they do not have essences, and therefore they resist classical phenomenological analysis.[23] We can cede the point that for complex cultural objects, history sometimes fills in the imaginative variation better than we can through free variation. In this way, history can aid the phenomenological exhibition of essences. Regarding the essential structure of experience, however, Foucault's claim is absurd and self-defeating. He says that it is a feature of the field of experience that what comes to light is bound to history. But this very claim, if it is true, transcends the idiosyncrasies of history. And the phenomenological analysis of the structured field of experience, of terms such as world, flesh, speech, truth, life, love, and wonder, are not idiosyncratic. They are, rather, essential features of our having experience. We might not always fathom them but they are necessarily there in the background making experience possible. Foucault's critique of phenomenology fails to distinguish everyday essences from the transcendental essence of experience, and this prevents him from realizing that attention to history does not undermine phenomenology's principal concern.

Deconstruction and the postmodern philosophy it inspires preserve the fundamental openness that constitutes phenomenology, but they upend this openness surreptitiously insofar as they deny the orientation of this openness to the transformative, transfiguring, truth of things.

Looking Forward

Husserl remains a touch obsessed with the idea of making the study of experience into a science. Of course, there's nothing wrong with this as an idea if science is understood to be an evidence-based investigation, but Husserl wants to achieve modern ideals of certitude in the face of radical doubt and he does so by hammering home, again and again, the priority of the self as agent of experience. He remains mired in some of the modern lingo of subjectivity that presents unnecessary barriers to the beginner. It can give the erroneous impression that phenomenology single-mindedly investigates the ego and nothing besides, whereas a closer study reveals that its novelty resides precisely in the way that it explodes the modern ego, as Heidegger puts it.[24]

Heidegger remedies this neglect in Husserl, but at the same time he can never settle on a technical vocabulary; instead, he produces neologism after neologism in work after work even though, at bottom, he is always trying to say the same thing about the same. The proliferation of technical terms presents unnecessary barriers to the beginner. It is also the case that Heidegger remains oriented exclusively toward an investigation of the basic structures of the understanding of being. That's a wonderful focus, but it is not the only thing phenomenology can investigate; Heidegger presents his narrow vision as a comprehensive vision, and as a result, one cannot help but feel cramped by his analyses.

Phenomenology is strongest as a collaborative movement. That's what Husserl originally envisioned, but he remained inflexible and could not see the value of the individual contributions of others. We are in a position to do better. We can gather together the insights of Husserl, Heidegger, and others so that we can see what they give us to see, understand what they give us to understand, and philosophize anew with a radicality that rivals that of Socrates. Such contemporary phenomenologists as Robert Sokolowski, Jean-Luc Marion, Mark Wrathall, Shaun Gallagher, and Dan Zahavi demonstrate phenomenology's continued fruitfulness in dialogue with contemporary philosophy of mind, philosophy of language, and philosophy of religion.

Today we are suspicious of our ability to arrive at truths that transcend us. With the paltry, putrid, pitiful account of experience at hand we have every reason to think that we cannot be receptive to things but instead must confect them. Phenomenology's great merit is to give us a robust account of experience in which the truths of things and essences can come to light. In constituting things, we let them be; that is, we free ourselves up to receive the things that are as they are. How is this possible?

Experience takes place in a shared *world* of presence. Our *flesh* installs each of us in this world together with others, thereby establishing the interplay of things being present to us and absent from us. *Speech*, which begins in presence, opens us up to a world of far-flung absences. *Truth* arises as the confirmation of what is said with what is experienced in the flesh. Human *life* is the unique mode of living in the truth of things. *Love* opens us up to the beloved and allows us to share intensely one and the same understanding of things. *Wonder* awakens us to the depths of experience and leads us to the truth of things.

Phenomenology invites us to awaken to the joy dulled down by habit, to recover and renew the riches of experience, which does not close us in on ourselves, but throws open a world of dazzling things. The phenomenological method allows us to wonder about the essence of experience and the experience of essences; it clarifies how transcendent truths arise thanks to our own act of transcendence. The phenomenological movement comes from all those who endeavor to go against the grain and hold themselves in the turbulent tumult of questioning experience. It comes from all those who, like Husserl, know the thrill of loving the truth of things:

> Love—loving, loses itself in the other, lives in the other, unites itself with the other, is wholly and entirely not hedonistic, although it establishes joys, "high" joys.[25]

GLOSSARY

Absence
Something's being hidden to one's flesh; contrasted with *presence*.

Adumbration
The way perceptual objects appear in experience through a continual interplay of present and absent sides; each appearance is an adumbration, or shadow cast by the thing as we explore it.

Alienation
The experience of distance between self and other; contrasted with *participation*.

Ambient energy
This sort of energy is configured by the contours of a thing and thereby it can convey the appearances of that thing to an observer; contrasted with *radiant energy*.

Appearances
The various ways in which one and the same thing comes to presence.

Authentic
A mode of experience marked by careful commitment to uncovering the truth of things and oneself; contrasted with *inauthentic*.

Being-in-the-world
A defining feature of human experience, naming the fact that it does not take place in our heads but instead out there among things with others.

Being-with
A defining feature of human experience, naming the fact that it is not individualistic but instead essentially communal.

Boredom
The fundamental mood of our day, which is defined by an indifference to all things occasioned by the eclipse of *wonder*.

Categorial intuition
The way in which we experience not only isolated perceptual objects but the relations that obtain between things; we see not only S and not only p, but we can see S *is* p, not only *cat* and not only *mat* but the cat's *being on* the mat.

Constitution
The activity of experience that lets the experienced thing appear as it is.

Dasein
Human existence, the technical term for the human being as both that for whom the world of experience happens and part of the world of experience; it combines *transcendental ego* and *empirical ego* to name the unified human being.

Difference in degree
A difference in degree is a quantitative difference in complexity in which the higher and the lower can be explained in terms of the same principles; contrasted with *difference in kind*.

Difference in kind
A difference in kind is a qualitative difference in which the higher cannot be explained in terms of the same principles that explain the lower; contrasted with *difference in degree*.

Eidetic intuition
A method for clarifying what something is (*eidos* in Greek) by exhibiting its essential features through a process of imaginative variation.

Empirical ego
The self as experienced (say, seeing *your hand* in the field of vision) as opposed to the self that experiences (say, *seeing* the field of vision), which is called the *transcendental ego*.

Environment
The context of surrounding things circumscribed by animal interests; contrasted with *world*.

Epoché
The process of taking theories, whether scientific or philosophical, as suggestions for personal investigation and possible confirmation or correction rather than as established facts.

Essence
What something is, its defining or identifying features, which distinguishes it from everything else.

Experience
The presencing and absencing of things.

Flesh
The living body as the experienced agent of experience; it instantiates our point of view in the world and makes that point of view available to the views of others.

Formal indication
The way ordinary words are repurposed by phenomenology to indicate phenomenological analyses that everyone must perform for oneself. These analyses are not interested in the ordinary content of experience but instead in its formal structure.

Human existence
The entity who stands open to the truth of things; it translates the German word *Dasein*.

Inauthentic
A mode of experience marked by careless superficiality and indifference to the task of uncovering the truth of things and oneself; contrasted with *authentic*.

Intentionality
Names the fact that experience experiences what is other than itself and that it does so in view of a particular understanding that can subsequently be put into words (experiencing the paper *as* paper allows us to say, "The paper *is* white").

Life
The power to transcend, marked on the lowest level by metabolism, in the case of animals by openness to an environment of desire and action, and in the case of humans also an openness to the world of truth and goodness.

Lifeworld
The specifically human qualitative domain of everyday things and perception, which serves as the ground for language and human life together as well as for quantitative inquiry.

Love
The intentional relation that allows us to see the beloved just as the beloved is and to share the beloved's world.

Method
The way to access the experience of things in their essence; the transcendental reduction accesses the essence of experience and eidetic intuition accesses the essence of things.

Mystery
Thoughtful participation in something that cannot be objectified and mastered because it includes us; contrasted with *problem*.

Natural attitude
The default ordinary mode of experience that focuses on things rather than their presence; contrasted with *phenomenological attitude*.

Ordo amoris
The order of love, which is both descriptive and prescriptive; as descriptive, it accounts for the horizon of interest a given person has in the world, a horizon that is open to others in love and is contagious; as prescriptive, it sketches the horizon of interest a person has who has abandoned all illusions that typically infect the descriptive.

Participation
The experience of nearness with others; contrasted with *alienation*.

Phenomenological attitude
The extraordinary mode of experience that focuses on presence and absence rather than things; contrasted with *natural attitude*.

Phenomenology
The study of how truth and essences arise in experience.

Presence
Something's being unhidden to one's flesh; contrasted with *absence*.

Problem
Something that can be objectified and mastered because it does not include us; contrasted with *mystery*.

Radiant energy
This sort of energy enters the observer directly from its source; because it is not configured by the contours of a thing, it does not convey any appearances; contrasted with *ambient energy*.

Shame
The experience of alienation, of becoming made into a public spectacle, of being reduced to a merely bodily being rather than a person or point of view on the whole.

Solidarity
The experience of *participation* in which one feels oneself to be a meaningful part of a social whole.

Transcendence
The activity of going beyond our prior conceptions in order to experience things and let them appear as they are.

Transcendental ego
The self that experiences (say, *seeing* the field of vision), as opposed to the self as experienced (say, seeing *your hand* in the field of vision), which is called the *empirical ego*.

Transcendental reduction
The return to experience, that is, the shift in focus from things to the experience of things.

Transcendent truths
Things, such as essences and mathematical equations, that are as they are independent of our experiencing them.

Truth
Confirmation: the experience of something's being just as it is understood to be.

Wonder
The origin of philosophy and the antidote to the restless *boredom* fueled by today's distraction devices; wonder primes us to enter more deeply into experience to uncover the truth of things and ourselves.

World
The domain of human experience, a domain that makes possible our encountering the truth of things together with others; contrasted with *environment*.

NOTES

Preface

1. Arthur Conan Doyle, "A Case of Identity," in *The Adventures of Sherlock Holmes* (New York: Harper & Brothers, 1904), 66. Emphasis added.

2. Heidegger, "My Way to Phenomenology," trans. Joan Stambaugh, in *On Time and Being* (New York: Harper & Row, 1972), 75. Emphasis added.

3. John Paul II, "To a Delegation of the World Institute of Phenomenology of Hanover," March 22, 2003, https://w2.vatican.va/content/john-paul-ii/en/speeches/2003/march/documents/hf_jp-ii_spe_20030322_hanover.html. Emphasis added.

4. Maurice Merleau-Ponty, *Phenomenology of Perception*, trans. Donald A. Landes (New York: Routledge, 2012), lxxxv.

Chapter 1

1. Stephen Hawking and Leonard Mlodinow, *The Grand Design* (New York: Bantam Books, 2010), 5.

2. Hawking and Mlodinow, *The Grand Design*, 5.

3. Hawking and Mlodinow, *The Grand Design*, 9, emphasis added.

4. Hawking and Mlodinow, *The Grand Design*, 32.

5. Hawking and Mlodinow, *The Grand Design*, 47.

6. Heidegger, "The Age of the World Picture," in *The Question Concerning Technology and Other Essays*, trans. William Lovitt (New York: Harper & Row, 1977), 130.

7. Hawking and Mlodinow, *The Grand Design*, 5.

8. For the previous two points, I am indebted to Alva Noë's perceptive analysis in *Infinite Baseball: Notes from a Philosopher at the Ballpark* (Oxford: Oxford University Press, 2019), 42–44.

9. Husserl, *Crisis of European Sciences and Transcendental Phenomenology: An Introduction to Phenomenological Philosophy*, trans. David Carr (Evanston, IL: Northwestern University Press, 1970), 285.

10. Husserl, *The Crisis*, 302: "The Socratic return to self-evidence represents a reaction; and specifically this is making clear to oneself, by means of example, the fields of pure possibilities the free variation which upholds the identity of meaning, identity of the object as substrate of determination, and makes it possible to discern this identity." See also *Ideas Pertaining to a Pure*

Phenomenology and to a Phenomenological Philosophy, Third Book: Phenomenology and the Foundations of the Sciences, trans. Ted. E. Klein and William E. Pohl (The Hague: Martinus Nijhoff, 1980), hereafter *Ideas III*, 86.

11. For the importance of the modern heritage, see Chad Engelland, *Heidegger's Shadow: Husserl, Kant, and the Transcendental Turn* (New York: Routledge, 2017).

12. Husserl, *Logical Investigations*, trans. F. N. Findlay (New York: Routledge, 2001), vol. 2, 76.

13. Husserl, *Logical Investigations*, vol. 2, 76.

14. Nietzsche, "Truth and Lies in a Nonmoral Sense," in *Philosophy and Truth: Selections from Nietzsche's Notebooks of the Early 1870s*, ed. and trans. Daniel Breazeale (Amherst, NY: Humanity Books, 1979), 86–87.

15. Preface to the second edition of *The Gay Science*, in *Portable Nietzsche*, ed. and trans. Walter Kaufmann (New York: Viking Penguin, 1954), p. 38.

16. Heidegger, *History of the Concept of Time: Prolegomena*, trans. Theodore Kisiel (Bloomington: Indiana University Press, 1985), 71.

17. Husserl, *Logical Investigations*, vol. 1, 175.

18. Heidegger, *History of the Concept of Time*, 76. Translation modified.

19. Max Scheler, "Phenomenology and the Theory of Cognition," in *Selected Philosophical Essays*, trans. David R. Lachterman (Evanston, IL: Northwestern University Press, 1973), 138.

Chapter 2

1. Husserl, *Logical Investigations*, vol. 2, 211.

2. Merleau-Ponty, "Eye and Mind," trans. Carleton Dallery, in *The Primacy of Perception*, ed. James M. Edie (Evanston, IL: Northwestern University Press, 1964), 180.

3. Husserl, *Cartesian Meditations: An Introduction to Phenomenology*, trans. Dorion Cairns (The Hague: Martinus Nijhoff, 1977), 111.

4. Hume, *Enquiry Concerning Human Understanding*, in *Enquiries*, 3rd ed., ed. L. A Selby-Bigge and P. H. Nidditch (Oxford: Clarendon Press, 1975), section 12, part 1.

5. Hume, *Enquiry*, section 12, part 1.

6. Hume, *Enquiry*, section 12, part 1.

7. Husserl, *Ideas for a Pure Phenomenology and Phenomenological Philosophy. First Book: General Introduction to Pure Phenomenology*, trans. Daniel Dahlstrom (Indianapolis, IN: Hackett, 2014), hereafter *Ideas I*, 72–73.

8. Husserl, *Ideas I*, 73. Translated modified.

9. Husserl, *Cartesian Meditations*, 147.

10. Husserl, *Ideas I*, 80.

11. Hawking and Mlodinow, *The Grand Design*, 46.

12. Nietzsche, "Truth and Lies in a Nonmoral Sense," 83–85.

13. Searle, *Intentionality* (Cambridge: Cambridge University Press, 1983), 230. My emphasis.

14. Sokolowski, *Phenomenology of the Human Person* (New York: Cambridge University Press, 2008), 198–200.

15. Sokolowski, *Phenomenology of the Human Person*, 225–237.

16. Heidegger, *Being and Time*, 98–99.

17. Heidegger, *The Fundamental Concepts of Metaphysics*, 177.

18. Heidegger, *History of the Concept of Time*, 196–197.

19. Husserl, *Cartesian Meditations*, 151.

Chapter 3

1. Merleau-Ponty, "Eye and Mind," 168.

2. See Paul Bloom, *How Children Learn the Meaning of Words* (Cambridge, MA: MIT Press, 2000).

3. Merleau-Ponty, "The Child's Relations with Others," trans. William Cobb, in *The Primacy of Perception*, 118.

4. Descartes, *Meditations on First Philosophy*, meditation 2, and *Discourse on Method*, part 5.

5. Scheler, *The Nature of Sympathy*, trans. Peter Heath (New Brunswick, NJ: Transaction, 2008), 256.

6. Heidegger, *Being and Time*, trans. John Macquarrie and Edward Robinson (New York: Harper & Row, 1962), 149–168.

7. Stein, *The Problem of Empathy*, 3rd ed., trans. Waltraut Stein (Washington, DC: ICS Publications, 1989), 71.

8. Husserl, *Cartesian Meditations*, 117.

9. Merleau-Ponty, *The Visible and the Invisible*, ed. Claude Lefort, trans. Alphonso Lingis (Evanston, IL: Northwestern University Press, 1968), 263. Translation modified.

10. Merleau-Ponty, "An Unpublished Text by Maurice Merleau-Ponty: A Prospectus of His Work," trans. Arleen B. Dallery, in *The Primacy of Perception*, 5.

11. Merleau-Ponty, "Eye and Mind," 170.

Chapter 4

1. Husserl writes that "the word *Löwe* [lion] occurs only once in the German language." *Crisis*, 357.

2. See Chad Engelland, *Ostension: Word Learning and the Embodied Mind* (Cambridge, MA: MIT Press, 2014).

3. Merleau-Ponty, *Phenomenology of Perception*, 422.

4. Husserl, *Logical Investigations*, vol. 2, 276.

5. Heidegger, *History of the Concept of Time*, 47.

6. Heidegger, *History of the Concept of Time*, 47.

7. I am grateful to Bill Frank for this point.

8. Gerard Manley Hopkins, "Pied Beauty," in *Poems of Gerard Manley Hopkins*, ed. Robert Bridges (London: Humphrey Milford, 1918), 30.

9. Sokolowski, *Phenomenology of the Human Person*, 48–67.

10. Husserl, *Logical Investigations*, vol. 2, 195.

11. Husserl, *Logical Investigations*, vol. 2, 280–281.

12. Husserl, *Logical Investigations*, vol. 2, 202.

13. Husserl, *Pathmarks*, ed. William McNeill (Cambridge: Cambridge University Press, 1998), 59.

Chapter 5

1. Nietzsche, *Will to Power*, trans. Walter Arnold Kaufmann and R. J. Hollingdale (New York: Random House, 1968), n. 515. My emphasis.

2. Husserl, *Ideas I*, 38.

3. Husserl, *Logical Investigations*, vol. 2, 261.

4. Merleau-Ponty, *The Prose of the World*, ed. Claude Lefort, trans. John O'Neill (Evanston, IL: Northwestern University Press, 1973), 129.

5. Husserl, *Logical Investigations*, vol. 2, 318.

6. Heidegger, *Being and Time*, 57.

7. Heidegger, *Introduction to Metaphysics*, 107.

8. Searle, "The Phenomenological Illusion," in *Erfahrung und Analyse*, ed. Maria E. Reicher and Johann Christian Marek (Vienna: ÖBV & HPT, 2005), 323.

9. Heidegger, *History of the Concept of Time*, 4.

10. Heidegger, *Becoming Heidegger: On the Trial of His Early Occasional Writings, 1910–1927*, ed. Theodore Kisiel and Thomas Sheehan (Evanston, IL: Northwestern University Press, 2007), 288.

11. Aristotle, *Metaphysics*, in *The Basic Works of Aristotle*, ed. Richard McKeon (New York: Random House, 1941), 9.10, 1051b7–9.

12. Husserl, *Logical Investigations*, vol. 2, 266.

13. Heidegger, *Towards the Definition of Philosophy*, trans. Ted Sadler (London: Athlone Press, 2000), 188.

Chapter 6

1. Michel Henry, *Barbarism*, trans. Scott Davidson (New York: Continuum, 2012), 6–7.

2. Stein, *On the Problem of Empathy*, 87.

3. Heidegger, *The Fundamental Concepts of Metaphysics*, trans. William McNeill and Nicholas Walker (Bloomington: Indiana University Press, 1995), 177.

4. Heidegger, *Fundamental Concepts*, 264.

5. Tomasello, *Origins of Human Communication* (Cambridge, MA: MIT Press, 2008), 37–38, citing Juan-Carlos Gomez, *Apes, Monkeys, Children, and the Growth of Mind* (Cambridge, MA: Harvard University Press, 2004).

6. Nietzsche, *Beyond Good and Evil: Prelude to a Philosophy of the Future*, trans. Walter Kaufmann (New York: Vintage Books, 1966), 46.

7. Derrida, *The Animal That Therefore I Am*, ed. Marie-Luise Mallet, trans. David Wills. (New York: Fordham University Press, 2008), 160.

8. Heidegger, *Being and Time*, 235–241.

9. See Steve Crowell, *Normativity and Phenomenology in Husserl and Heidegger* (Cambridge: Cambridge University Press, 2013).

10. See Chad Engelland, "Heidegger and the Human Difference," *Journal of the American Philosophical Association* 1 (2015): 175–193.

11. Husserl, *The Crisis*, 3–189; Heidegger, "Building, Dwelling, Thinking," trans. Albert Hofstadter, in *Basic Writings*, ed. David Farrell Krell (New York: HarperCollins, 1993), 347–363.

12. Hans Jonas, *The Phenomenon of Life: Toward a Philosophical Biology* (Evanston, IL: Northwestern University Press, 2001), 83–86. Following Jonas, Leon Kass works out the web of significance at work in the full humanization of the animal need to eat. See *The Hungry Soul: Eating and the Perfecting of Our Nature* (Chicago: University of Chicago Press, 1999).

13. "Inside a Great Mind," *Parade Magazine*, https://parade.com/37704/parade/12-inside-a-great-mind/.

14. Mark Kurzem, *The Mascot: Unraveling the Mystery of My Jewish Father's Nazi Boyhood* (New York: Viking Penguin, 2007), 58.

15. Levinas, *Ethics and Infinity: Conversations with Philippe Nemo*, trans. Richard Cohen (Pittsburgh, PA: Duquesne University Press, 1995), 87.

16. Marcel, *The Mystery of Being*, vol. 1, trans. G. S. Fraser (South Bend, IN: St. Augustine's Press, 2001), 216–217.

17. Levinas, *Totality and Infinity: An Essay on Exteriority*, trans. Alphonso Lingis (Pittsburgh, PA: Duquesne University Press, 1969), 200.

Chapter 7

1. Heidegger, *History of the Concept of Time*, 296. Dietrich von Hildebrand says mistaking love for an urge "is surely the most radical misconception of the nature of love." *The Nature of Love*, trans. John F. Crosby with John Henry Crosby (South Bend, IN: St. Augustine's Press, 2009), 25.

2. https://w2.vatican.va/content/john-paul-ii/en/speeches/2003/march/documents/hf_jp-ii_spe_20030322_hanover.html.

3. Heidegger, *Pathmarks*, 87. Translation modified.

4. Merleau-Ponty, *Phenomenology of Perception*, 429.

5. Nietzsche, *Beyond Good and Evil*, 93.

6. Scheler, *Selected Philosophical Essays*, 110–111.

7. Scheler, *Selected Philosophical Essays*, 110.

8. Scheler, *Selected Philosophical Essays*, 127.

9. Scheler, *Selected Philosophical Essays*, 124.

10. Scheler, *Ressentiment*, trans. Lewis B. Coser and William W. Holdheim (Milwaukee, WI: Marquette University Press, 2007), 87

11. Scheler, *Ressentiment*, 87.

12. Scheler, *Selected Philosophical Writings*, 113.

13. Marion, *The Erotic Phenomenon*, trans. Stephen E. Lewis (Chicago: University of Chicago Press, 2007), 22.

14. Sartre, *Being and Nothingness: An Essay on Phenomenological Ontology*, trans. Hazel E. Barnes (New York: Philosophical Library, 1970), 255.

15. Sartre, *Being and Nothingness*, 262.

16. Scheler, *Person and Self-Value: Three Essays*, trans. M. S. Frings (Dordrecht: Martinus Nijhoff, 1987), 17.

17. Scheler, *Person and Self-Value*, 18.

18. *FCC v. AT&T Inc.*, 562 U.S. 397 (2011).

19. Scheler, *Person and Self-Value*, 11.

20. Merleau-Ponty, *Phenomenology of Perception*, 169–170.

21. Wojtyła, *Love and Responsibility* (San Francisco: Ignatius Press, 1981), 174–193.

22. Merleau-Ponty, *Phenomenology of Perception*, 376.

23. Heidegger, *Being and Time*, 206.

24. Wojtyła, *The Acting Person*, ed. Anna-Teresa Tymieniecka, trans. Andrzej Potocki, in *Analecta Husserliana: The Yearbook of Phenomenological Research, X* (Dordrecht: D. Reidel, 1979), 337–348.

Chapter 8

1. Gadamer, *Truth and Method*, 2nd, rev. ed., trans. Joel Weinsheimer and Donald G. Marshall (New York: Continuum, 1989), 101–110.

2. Heidegger, "Origin of the Work of Art," trans. Albert Hofstadter, in *Basic Writings*, ed. David Farrell Krell (New York: HarperCollins, 1993), 206.

3. Heidegger, *What Is Called Thinking?*, trans. J. Glenn Gray (New York: Harper & Row, 1968), 5. Translation modified.

4. Heidegger, *Fundamental Concepts of Metaphysics*, 77.

5. Heidegger, *Discourse on Thinking*, trans. John M. Anderson and E. Hans Freund (New York: Harper & Row, 1966), 53–54.

6. Marcel, *Mystery of Being*, vol. 1, 18–38, and vol. 2, 42, respectively

7. Marcel, *Mystery of Being*, vol. 1, 197–219; Merleau-Ponty, *Phenomenology of Perception*, lxxxv.

8. Heidegger, *Basic Questions of Philosophy: Selected "Problems" of "Logic,"* trans. Richard Rojcewicz and André Schuwer (Bloomington: Indiana University Press, 1994), §§36–38.

9. Heidegger, *Fundamental Concepts of Metaphysics*, 190.

10. JoAnna Klein, "Why Do Zebras Have Stripes? Scientists Camouflaged Horses to Find Out," https://www.nytimes.com/2019/02/20/science/zebra-stripes-flies.html.

11. Heidegger, "What Is Metaphysics?," in *Pathmarks*, 95–96.

12. Quoted in Christy Marx, *Grace Hopper: The First Woman to Program the First Computer in the United States* (New York: Rosen Publishing Group, 2004), 77.

13. https://www.merriam-webster.com/words-at-play/top-10-most-frequently-looked-up-words/love.

14. On the essence of friendship, see Aristotle, *Nicomachean Ethics*, books 8 and 9.

15. Husserl, *Crisis*, 285.

16. Husserl, *Crisis*, 165.

17. Aristotle, *Nicomachean Ethics*, book 9, chapter 9.

18. Aristotle, *Rhetoric*, in *The Basic Works of Aristotle*, 1.11, 1370b22–24.

19. Augustine, *Confessions*, trans. Henry Chadwick (Oxford: Oxford University Press, 1991), 60–61.

20. Heidegger, *The Basic Problems of Phenomenology*, rev. ed., trans. Albert Hofstadter (Bloomington: Indiana University Press, 1982), 328.

Chapter 9

1. Augustine, *Confessions*, 230–231.

2. Husserl, *Shorter Works*, ed. Peter McCormick and Frederick A. Elliston (Notre Dame, IN: University of Notre Dame Press, 1981), 196.

3. Heidegger, *Fundamental Concepts of Metaphysics*, 293–300.

4. Husserl, *Ideas I*, 33.

5. Heidegger, *Basic Problems of Phenomenology*, 23.

6. Heidegger, *Being and Time*, 492.

7. Augustine, *Confessions*, book 1, chapter 20, and book 10, chapters 30–42.

8. Heidegger, *History of the Concept of Time*, 56.

9. Husserl, *Crisis*, 362.

10. On confirmation as removal of quotation marks, see Sokolowski, *Introduction to Phenomenology* (New York: Cambridge University Press, 2000), 187–188.

11. I am grateful to Chris Mirus for this point.

12. Heidegger, *The Phenomenology of Religious Life*, trans. Matthias Fritsch and Jennifer Anna Gosetti-Ferencei (Bloomington: Indiana University Press, 2004), 13.

13. Heidegger, *Being and Time*, 230.

14. Scheler, *Formalism in Ethics and Non-Formal Ethics of Values: A New Attempt toward the Foundation of an Ethical Personalism*, trans. Manfred S. Frings and Roger L. Funk (Evanston, IL: Northwestern University Press, 1973), 71-72.

15. Heidegger, *Being and Time*, 237.

Chapter 10

1. For an extended defense of the positive relation of Husserl and Heidegger, see Engelland, *Heidegger's Shadow: Husserl, Kant, and the Transcendental Turn*.

2. Scheler, *Selected Philosophical Writings*, 137.

3. Husserl, *Ideas I*, 116.

4. Husserl, *Crisis*, 166.

5. Heidegger, *Being and Time*, 490.

6. Husserl, *Psychological and Transcendental Phenomenology*, 270. Translation modified.

7. Husserl, *Psychological and Transcendental Phenomenology*, 284.

8. Heidegger, *Becoming Heidegger*, 326. Translation modified.

9. For this suggestion, see the translator's introduction to Heidegger, *Logic: The Question of Truth*, trans. Thomas Sheehan (Bloomington: Indiana University Press, 2010), xi.

10. Husserl, *Ideas I*, 114.

11. Heidegger, *Basic Questions*, 178.

12. Rudolf Carnap, "The Elimination of Metaphysics through Logical Analysis of Language," trans. Arthur Pap, in *Logical Positivism*, ed. A. J. Ayer (Glencoe, IL: Free Press, 1959), 69.

13. Husserl, *The Idea of Phenomenology*, 46.

14. Heidegger, *History of the Concept of Time*, 146.

15. See Richard Polt, *Time and Trauma: Thinking through Heidegger in the Thirties* (London: Rowman & Littlefield, 2019).

16. See Dietrich von Hildebrand, *My Battle against Hitler: Defiance in the Shadow of the Third Reich,* trans. John Henry Crosby (New York: Image Books, 2016).

17. Husserl, *Ideas III*, 76.

18. Sartre, "Existentialism," trans. Benard Frechtman, in *Existentialism and Human Emotions* (New York: Carol Publishing, 1993), 23.

19. Heidegger, *Pathmarks*, 271.

20. Heidegger, *Pathmarks*, 250.

21. Heidegger's letter to William J. Richardson, April 1962, in "Preface" to William J. Richardson, *Heidegger: Through Phenomenology to Thought*, 2nd ed. (The Hague: Martinus Nijhoff, 1967), xvi.

22. Gadamer, *Truth and Method*, 576.

23. Foucault, *Archaeology of Knowledge*, trans. A. M. Sheridan Smith (New York: Pantheon Books, 1972), 61.

24. Heidegger, *Phenomenology of Religious Life*, 36.

25. Husserl, *Zur Phänomenologie der Intersubjektivität. Texte aus dem Nachlass. Dritter Teil: 1929–1935*, ed. Iso Kern (The Hague: Martinus Nijhoff, 1973), 406.

BIBLIOGRAPHY

Aristotle. *The Basic Works of Aristotle*. Ed. Richard McKeon. New York: Random House, 1941.

Augustine. *Confessions*. Trans. Henry Chadwick. Oxford: Oxford University Press, 1991.

Bloom, Paul. *How Children Learn the Meaning of Words*. Cambridge, MA: MIT Press, 2000.

Carnap, Rudolf. "The Elimination of Metaphysics through Logical Analysis of Language." Trans. Arthur Pap. In *Logical Positivism*, ed. A. J. Ayer (Glencoe, IL: Free Press, 1959.

Crowell, Steven. *Normativity and Phenomenology in Husserl and Heidegger*. Cambridge: Cambridge University Press, 2013.

Derrida, Jacques. *The Animal That Therefore I Am*. Ed. Marie-Luise Mallet. Trans. David Wills. New York: Fordham University Press, 2008.

Engelland, Chad. "Heidegger and the Human Difference." *Journal of the American Philosophical Association* 1 (2015): 175–193.

Engelland, Chad. *Heidegger's Shadow: Husserl, Kant, and the Transcendental Turn*. New York: Routledge, 2017.

Engelland, Chad. *Ostension: World Learning and the Embodied Mind*. Cambridge, MA: MIT Press, 2014.

Gadamer, Hans-Georg. *Truth and Method*, 2nd, rev. ed. Trans. Joel Weinsheimer and Donald G. Marshall. New York: Continuum, 1989.

Gomez, Juan-Carlos. *Apes, Monkeys, Children, and the Growth of Mind*. Cambridge, MA: Harvard University Press, 2004.

Hawking, Stephen, and Leonard Mlodinow. *The Grand Design*. New York: Bantam Books, 2010.

Heidegger, Martin. *The Basic Problems of Phenomenology*, rev. ed. Trans. Albert Hofstadter. Bloomington: Indiana University Press, 1982.

Heidegger, Martin. *Basic Questions of Philosophy: Selected "Problems" of "Logic."* Trans. Richard Rojcewicz and André Schuwer. Bloomington: Indiana University Press, 1994.

Heidegger, Martin. *Becoming Heidegger: On the Trial of His Early Occasional Writings, 1910–1927.* Ed. Theodore Kisiel and Thomas Sheehan. Evanston, IL: Northwestern University Press, 2007.

Heidegger, Martin. *Being and Time.* Trans. John Macquarrie and Edward Robinson. New York: Harper & Row, 1962.

Heidegger, Martin. "Building, Dwelling, Thinking." Trans. Albert Hofstadter. In *Basic Writings*, ed. David Farrell Krell, 347–363. New York: HarperCollins, 1993.

Heidegger, Martin. *Discourse on Thinking.* Trans. John M. Anderson and E. Hans Freund. New York: Harper & Row, 1966.

Heidegger, Martin. *The Fundamental Concepts of Metaphysics.* Trans. William McNeill and Nicholas Walker. Bloomington: Indiana University Press, 1995.

Heidegger, Martin. *History of the Concept of Time: Prolegomena.* Trans. Theodore Kisiel. Bloomington: Indiana University Press, 1985.

Heidegger, Martin. *Introduction to Metaphysics.* Trans. Gregory Fried and Richard Polt. New Haven: Yale University Press, 2000.

Heidegger, Martin. "Letter to William J. Richardson, April 1962." In "Preface" to William J. Richardson, *Heidegger: Through Phenomenology to Thought*, 2nd ed. The Hague: Martinus Nijhoff, 1967.

Heidegger, Martin. *Logic: The Question of Truth.* Trans. Thomas Sheehan. Bloomington: Indiana University Press, 2010.

Heidegger, Martin. "My Way to Phenomenology." Trans. Joan Stambaugh. In *On Time and Being*, 74–82. New York: Harper & Row, 1972.

Heidegger, Martin. "Origin of the Work of Art." Trans. Albert Hofstadter. In *Basic Writings*, ed. David Farrell Krell, 143–212. New York: HarperCollins, 1993.

Heidegger, Martin. *Pathmarks.* Ed. William McNeill. Cambridge: Cambridge University Press, 1998.

Heidegger, Martin. *The Phenomenology of Religious Life.* Trans. Matthias Fritsch and Jennifer Anna Gosetti-Ferencei. Bloomington: Indiana University Press, 2004.

Heidegger, Martin. *The Question Concerning Technology and Other Essays*. Trans. William Lovitt. New York: Harper & Row, 1977.

Heidegger, Martin. *Towards the Definition of Philosophy*. Trans. Ted Sadler. London: Athlone Press, 2000.

Heidegger, Martin. *What Is Called Thinking?* Trans. J. Glenn Gray. New York: Harper & Row, 1968.

Heidegger, Martin. *What Is a Thing?* Trans. William Barton and Vera Deutsch. Chicago: Henry Regnery Co., 1967.

Henry, Michel. *Barbarism*. Trans. Scott Davidson. New York: Continuum, 2012.

Hildebrand, Dietrich von. *My Battle against Hitler: Defiance in the Shadow of the Third Reich*. Trans. John Henry Crosby. New York: Image Books, 2016.

Hildebrand, Dietrich von. *The Nature of Love*. Trans. John F. Crosby with John Henry Crosby. South Bend, IN: St. Augustine's Press, 2009.

Hopkins, Gerard Manley. "Pied Beauty." In *Poems of Gerard Manley Hopkins*, ed. Robert Bridges. London: Humphrey Milford, 1918.

Hume, David. *Enquiry Concerning Human Understanding*. In *Enquiries*, 3rd ed. Ed. L. A Selby-Bigge and P. H. Nidditch. Oxford: Clarendon Press, 1975.

Husserl, Edmund. *Cartesian Meditations: An Introduction to Phenomenology*. Trans. Dorion Cairns. The Hague: Martinus Nijhoff, 1977.

Husserl, Edmund. *The Crisis of European Sciences and Transcendental Phenomenology: An Introduction to Phenomenological Philosophy*. Trans. David Carr. Evanston, IL: Northwestern University Press, 1970.

Husserl, Edmund. *The Idea of Phenomenology*. Trans. William P. Alston and George Nakhnikian. The Hague: Martinus Nijhoff, 1964.

Husserl, Edmund. *Ideas for a Pure Phenomenology and Phenomenological Philosophy. First Book: General Introduction to Pure Phenomenology*. Trans. Daniel Dahlstrom. Indianapolis, IN: Hackett, 2014.

Husserl, Edmund. *Ideas Pertaining to a Pure Phenomenology and to a Phenomenological Philosophy. Third Book: Phenomenology and the Foundations of the Sciences*. Trans. Ted. E. Klein and William E. Pohl. The Hague: Martinus Nijhoff, 1980.

Husserl, Edmund. *Logical Investigations*. Trans. F. N. Findlay. New York: Routledge, 2001.

Husserl, Edmund. *Psychological and Transcendental Phenomenology and the Confrontation with Heidegger (1927–1931)*. Ed. and trans. Thomas Sheehan and Richard Palmer. Dordrecht: Kluwer Academic, 1997.

Husserl, Edmund. *Shorter Works*. Ed. Peter McCormick and Frederick A. Elliston. Notre Dame, IN: University of Notre Dame Press, 1981.

Husserl, Edmund. *Zur Phänomenologie der Intersubjektivität. Texte aus dem Nachlass. Dritter Teil: 1929–1935*. Ed. Iso Kern. The Hague: Martinus Nijhoff, 1973.

Kurzem, Mark. *The Mascot: Unraveling the Mystery of My Jewish Father's Nazi Boyhood*. New York: Viking Penguin, 2007.

Levinas, Emmanuel. *Ethics and Infinity: Conversations with Philippe Nemo*. Trans. Richard Cohen. Pittsburgh, PA: Duquesne University Press, 1995.

Levinas, Emmanuel. *Totality and Infinity: An Essay on Exteriority*. Trans. Alphonso Lingis. Pittsburgh, PA: Duquesne University Press, 1969.

Marcel, Gabriel. *The Mystery of Being*, vol. 1. Trans. G. S. Fraser. South Bend, IN: St. Augustine's Press, 2001.

Marion, Jean-Luc. *The Erotic Phenomenon*. Trans. Stephen E. Lewis. Chicago: University of Chicago Press, 2007.

Marx, Christy. *Grace Hopper: The First Woman to Program the First Computer in the United States*. New York: Rosen Publishing Group, 2004.

Merleau-Ponty, Maurice. *The Phenomenology of Perception*. Trans. Donald A. Landes. New York: Routledge, 2012.

Merleau-Ponty, Maurice. *The Primacy of Perception*. Ed. James M. Edie. Evanston, IL: Northwestern University Press, 1964.

Merleau-Ponty, Maurice. *The Prose of the World*. Ed. Claude Lefort. Trans. John O'Neill. Evanston, IL: Northwestern University Press, 1973.

Merleau-Ponty, Maurice. *The Visible and the Invisible*. Ed. Claude Lefort. Trans. Alphonso Lingis. Evanston, IL: Northwestern University Press, 1968.

Nietzsche, Friedrich. *Beyond Good and Evil: Prelude to a Philosophy of the Future*. Trans. Walter Kaufmann. New York: Vintage Books, 1966.

Nietzsche, Friedrich. *Portable Nietzsche*. Ed. and trans. Walter Kaufmann. New York: Viking Penguin, 1954.

Nietzsche, Friedrich. "Truth and Lies in a Nonmoral Sense." In *Philosophy and Truth: Selections from Nietzsche's Notebooks of the Early 1870s*, ed. and trans. Daniel Breazeale. Amherst, NY: Humanity Books, 1979.

Nietzsche, Friedrich. *Will to Power*. Trans. Walter Arnold Kaufmann and R. J. Hollingdale. New York: Random House, 1968.

Noë, Alva. *Action in Perception*. Cambridge, MA: MIT Press, 2004.

Noë, Alva. *Infinite Baseball: Notes from a Philosopher at the Ballpark*. Oxford: Oxford University Press, 2019.

Polt, Richard. *Time and Trauma: Thinking through Heidegger in the Thirties*. London: Rowman & Littlefield, 2019.

Sartre, Jean-Paul. *Being and Nothingness: An Essay on Phenomenological Ontology*. Trans. Hazel E. Barnes. New York: Philosophical Library, 1970.

Sartre, Jean-Paul. "Existentialism." Trans. Benard Frechtman. In *Existentialism and Human Emotions*. New York: Carol Publishing, 1993.

Scheler, Max. *Formalism in Ethics and Non-Formal Ethics of Values: A New Attempt toward the Foundation of an Ethical Personalism*. Trans. Manfred S. Frings and Roger L. Funk. Evanston, IL: Northwestern University Press, 1973.

Scheler, Max. *The Nature of Sympathy*. Trans. Peter Heath. New Brunswick, NJ: Transaction, 2008.

Scheler, Max. *Person and Self-Value: Three Essays*. Trans. M. S. Frings. Dordrecht: Martinus Nijhoff, 1987.

Scheler, Max. *Selected Philosophical Essays*. Trans. David R. Lachterman. Evanston, IL: Northwestern University Press, 1973.

Searle, John. *Intentionality*. Cambridge: Cambridge University Press, 1983.

Searle, John. "The Phenomenological Illusion." In *Erfahrung und Analyse*, ed. Maria E. Reicher and Johann Christian Marek, 317–336. Vienna: ÖBV & HPT, 2005.

Sokolowski, Robert. *Introduction to Phenomenology*. New York: Cambridge University Press, 2000.

Sokolowski, Robert. *Phenomenology of the Human Person*. New York: Cambridge University Press, 2008.

Stein, Edith. *The Problem of Empathy*. 3rd ed. Trans. Waltraut Stein. Washington, DC: ICS Publications, 1989.

Tomasello, Michael. *Origins of Human Communication*. Cambridge, MA: MIT Press, 2008.

Wojtyła, Karol. *The Acting Person*. Ed. Anna-Teresa Tymieniecka. Trans. Andrzej Potocki. In *Analecta Husserliana: The Yearbook of Phenomenological Research, X*. Dordrecht: D. Reidel, 1979.

Wojtyła, Karol. *Love and Responsibility*. San Francisco: Ignatius Press, 1981.

FURTHER READING

Carman, Taylor. *Merleau-Ponty*. New York: Routledge, 2008.

Engelland, Chad. *Ostension: Word Learning and the Embodied Mind*. Cambridge, MA: MIT Press, 2014.

Gallagher, Shaun, and Dan Zahavi. *The Phenomenological Mind*. 2nd ed. New York: Routledge, 2012.

Heidegger, Martin. *History of the Concept of Time: Prolegomena*. Trans. Theodore Kisiel. Bloomington: Indiana University Press, 1985.

Husserl, Edmund. *The Crisis of European Sciences and Transcendental Phenomenology: An Introduction to Phenomenological Philosophy*. Trans. David Carr. Evanston, IL: Northwestern University Press, 1970.

Marcel, Gabriel. *The Mystery of Being*, vol. 1. Trans. G. S. Fraser. South Bend, IN: St. Augustine's Press, 2001.

Marion, Jean-Luc. *The Erotic Phenomenon*. Trans. Stephen E. Lewis. Chicago: University of Chicago Press, 2007.

Merleau-Ponty, Maurice. *The Phenomenology of Perception*. Trans. Donald A. Landes. New York: Routledge, 2012.

Mooney, Timothy, and Dermot Moran, eds. *The Phenomenology Reader*. New York: Routledge, 2002.

Moran, Dermot. *Introduction to Phenomenology*. New York: Routledge, 2000.

Sheehan, Thomas. *Heidegger's Being and Time: A New Reading*. London: Rowman & Littlefield, 2020.

Sokolowski, Robert. *Introduction to Phenomenology*. New York: Cambridge University Press, 2000.

Sokolowski, Robert. *Phenomenology of the Human Person*. New York: Cambridge University Press, 2008.

Wood, Robert E. *Being and Cosmos: From Seeing to Indwelling*. Washington, DC: Catholic University of America Press, 2018.

Wrathal, Mark. *How to Read Heidegger*. New York: W. W. Norton, 2005.

Zahavi, Dan. *Husserl's Phenomenology*. Stanford, CA: Stanford University Press, 2003.

INDEX

The MIT Press Essential Knowledge Series

CHAD ENGELLAND is Associate Professor of Philosophy and Chair of the Department of Philosophy at the University of Dallas. He is the author of *Ostension: Word Learning and the Embodied Mind* (MIT Press), *The Way of Philosophy: An Introduction*, and *Heidegger's Shadow: Kant, Husserl, and the Transcendental Turn*.